The Government Manager's Guide to Source Selection

The Government Manager's Essential Library

1. *The Government Manager's Guide to Appropriations Law,* William G. Arnold, CDFM-A
2. *The Government Manager's Guide to Source Selection,* Charles D. Solloway, Jr., CPCM
3. *The Government Manager's Guide to Contract Negotiation,* LeGette McIntyre
4. *The Government Manager's Guide to Plain Language,* Judith Gillespie Myers, Ph.D.
5. *The Government Manager's Guide to the Work Breakdown Structure,* Gregory T. Haugan, Ph.D., PMP
6. *The Government Manager's Guide to Strategic Planning,* Kathleen E. Monahan
7. *The Government Manager's Guide to Project Management,* Jonathan Weinstein, PMP and Timothy Jaques, PMP
8. *The Government Manager's Guide to Leading Teams,* Lisa DiTullio
9. *The Government Manager's Guide to Earned Value Management,* Charles I. Budd, PMP, and Charlene S. Budd, Ph.D., CPA, CMA, CFM, PMP
10. *The Government Manager's Guide to the Statement of Work,* Michael G. Martin, PMP
11. *The Government Manager's Guide to Contract Law,* Terrence O'Connor

The Government Manager's Guide to Source Selection

CHARLES D. SOLLOWAY, JR., CPCM

MANAGEMENTCONCEPTS PRESS

MANAGEMENTCONCEPTS PRESS

8230 Leesburg Pike, Suite 800
Tysons Corner, Virginia 22182
Phone: 703.790.9595
Fax: 703.790.1371
www.managementconcepts.com

Copyright © 2013 by Management Concepts Press, Inc.

All rights reserved. No part of this book may be reproduced or utilized in any form or by any means, electronic or mechanical, including photocopying, recording, or by an information storage and retrieval system, without permission in writing from the author and the publisher, except for brief quotations in review articles.

Printed in the United States of America

Library of Congress Control Number: 2013933651

ISBN 978-1-56726-401-2

Portions of this book have been adapted with permission from *Source Selection Step by Step: A Working Guide for Every Member of the Acquisition Team* by Charles D. Solloway, Jr., © 2011 by Management Concepts, Inc. All rights reserved.

ABOUT THE AUTHOR

Charles D. Solloway, Jr., CPCM, has more than 40 years of acquisition experience in the government and private sector. As a civilian employee of the U.S. Army, he held positions as buyer, contract specialist, contract negotiator, procurement analyst, contracting officer, director of contracting, and principal assistant responsible for contracting. Solloway twice received the U.S. Army's highest civilian award, the Decoration for Exceptional Civilian Service, for innovations in contracting.

He has authored or coauthored a number of textbooks, including the comprehensive *Source Selection Step by Step*, and has published many magazine articles on acquisition topics. He has taught thousands of acquisition professionals for private organizations such as Management Concepts, Inc.; for the federal government; and for institutions such as the Florida Institute of Technology.

A Certified Professional Contracts Manager (CPCM) and a Fellow of the National Contract Management Association (NCMA), Solloway serves on the NCMA Special Topic Committee on Contract Management Education.

To Doc and Marie Solloway

CONTENTS

PREFACE xvii

CHAPTER 1: Getting Everyone on Board 1
    The Vision 1
    The Stakeholders 1
    Coming to Consensus on an Acquisition Strategy 3
    The People and the Process 4

CHAPTER 2: An Overview of Source Selection 5
    Sole Source vs. Competition 5
    Competitive Source Selections 5
    Best Value 6
    FAR Source Selection Coverage 6
    Process Events 6

CHAPTER 3: Lowest Price, Technically Acceptable vs. Trade-Off 11
    Lowest Price, Technically Acceptable 11
    Trade-off 11
    A Practical Example 12
    Advantages and Disadvantages of LPTA 13
    Advantages and Disadvantages of Trade-off 14
    Agency Guidance 14

CHAPTER 4: The Acquisition Plan and the Source Selection Plan 15
    The Acquisition Plan 15
    The Acquisition Team 16
    The Source Selection Strategy 16
    The Contents of a Source Selection Plan 16
    Formats of the Acquisition Plan and Source Selection Plans ... 17

CHAPTER 5: Protests 21
Extraordinary Contractor Rights 21
The Stay Provisions 21
Override Procedures 21
Definition of a Protest 22
What Is an Interested Party? 22
Matters Addressed in Protests 23
Timeliness 23
When Interested Party or Timeliness Standards Are Not Met 23
Comptroller General Decision Times 24
Agency Responsibilities 24
Impact of Protests 24
Attorney Fees and Bid and Proposal Costs 25

CHAPTER 6: Organizing for Source Selection 27
The Source Selection Authority 27
Duties of the Source Selection Authority 27
The Role of the Contracting Officer 28
Evaluators 28
Formal and Other Than Formal Source Selection 28
Advisors 29
The Number of Evaluators and Advisors 30
The Origin of Evaluators and Advisors 30
Use of Contractors as Evaluators and Advisors 30
Competence and Fairness 31
Source Selection Rules 32

CHAPTER 7: Market Research 33
Requirements and Goals 33
The Smart Buyer Concept 34

Market Research Techniques 34
Documentation of Market Research 35

CHAPTER 8: Involving Contractors in Source Selection Planning 37
Contractor Participation Encouraged 37
Presolicitation Exchanges: Issues and Techniques 37

CHAPTER 9: Establishing Proposal Evaluation Factors 41
FAR Requirements 41
Evaluation Factors and Subfactors 42
Sample-itis 44
Great Latitude 44
Where to Begin 45

CHAPTER 10: Small Business Participation as a Merit Factor 47
Applicable FAR Clause Alternatives 47
Approved Subcontracting Plans 48
Agency Guidance 48
Small Disadvantaged Business Participation Program 48
Other Socioeconomic Evaluation Factors 49

CHAPTER 11: Establishing Proposal Evaluation Subfactors 51

CHAPTER 12: Establishing the Relative Importance of Evaluation Factors and Subfactors 53
Lowest Price, Technically Acceptable Excluded 53
Discretion of Planners 54
Describing Relative Importance 54
When Relative Importance Is Not Specified 55
The Impact of Relative Importance 55
What If? 56

CHAPTER 13: Selecting a Rating Method 57
Using Numbers 57

Using Adjectives or Colors 59
Variations on Common Rating Methods 59

CHAPTER 14: Past Performance as an Evaluation Factor 61
Past Performance vs. Experience 61
A Hard Nut to Crack 61
Addressing Concerns About the Use of Past Performance 62
Planning Concerns 63
FAR Guidance 64

CHAPTER 15: The Relative Importance of Cost 65
FAR Requirements 65
The Continuum of Importance 66

CHAPTER 16: Designing Proposal Preparation Instructions 67
Standard Practice 67
Variations 68
Media to Be Used 68
Issues to Consider 68
Use of Market Research 69

CHAPTER 17: Oral Presentations 71
An Opportunity for Dialogue 71
"Job Interview" 72
Pop Quizzes 72
Time for Presentations 72
Dialogue and Discussions 74

CHAPTER 18: Advertising a Planned Acquisition 75
Goals of the Synopsis Requirement 75
Exceptions to the Synopsis Requirement 76
Other Situations in Which Synopses Are Used 76
Combined Solicitation/Synopsis 77

CHAPTER 19: Preparing the Solicitation 79
Instructions to Offerors 80
Compatibility and Clarity 80
Special Standards 81
Careful Preparation and Proofreading 81
Making the Solicitation Available 81

CHAPTER 20: Holding a Preproposal Conference 89
Notifying Contractors of a Conference 89
Lack of FAR Guidance 89
Site Visits 90
Agency Practices 90
Preproposal Conference Task List 91

CHAPTER 21: Briefing Evaluators and Advisors 95

CHAPTER 22: Evaluating Merit/Technical Factors 99
Beginning Proposal Evaluations 99
A Typical Evaluation Process 99
Use of Agency Forms 102
Matching the Words with the Music 102
Retaining Evaluators and Retaining Evaluation Forms 102
Evaluating Small Business Subcontracting Plans 103

CHAPTER 23: Evaluating Past Performance 105
When There Is No Past Performance Information 106
Other Past Performance Evaluator Responsibilities 107

CHAPTER 24: Evaluating Proposed Cost or Price 109
FAR Preference 109
When Cost Analysis Is Essential 110
Cost Realism and Probable Cost 110
Technical Analysis of Cost Proposals 112

The Cost Evaluation Report 112
Participation in Discussions 112

CHAPTER 25: Clarifications and Award without Discussions 115
FAR Coverage on Clarifications.. 115
LPTA Contract Awards... 116
Changing the Award Approach 117

CHAPTER 26: Establishing the Competitive Range........................... 119
Avoiding Arbitrary Cutoff Points... 119
Inclusion of Unacceptable Proposals 120
Reductions for the Sake of Efficiency 120
Characteristics of the Competitive Range 120
A Subjective Decision 121

CHAPTER 27: The Exchange Known as Communications 123
FAR Coverage 123
When Communications Are Appropriate 123
Required Communications.. 124
Identifying the Need for Communications 124

CHAPTER 28: Holding Discussions 125
FAR Coverage of Discussions... 125
What Must Be Discussed 126
Discussing Cost or Price.. 126
The Need for Meaningful Discussions.. 127
The Manner and Specificity of Discussions.................................. 128
Contractor Alternatives in Discussions 128

CHAPTER 29: Prohibited Exchanges 131
Favoring.. 132
Protection of Proprietary Information 132
Limits on Cost and Price Exchanges.. 132

Limits on the Release of Past Performance Information 133
Protection of Source Selection Information 133

CHAPTER 30: Proposal Revisions **135**
Interim Revisions 135
Reopening Discussions 135
The BAFO and the BARFO 136
Evaluation After Final Proposal Revisions 137

CHAPTER 31: Making and Documenting the Source Selection Decision **139**
A Persuasive Sales Document 140
Quantifying the Decision 140
Documenting the Decision Without Quantification 141
Source Selection Records 141
Advice from Evaluators and Superiors 141
Trading Cost for Quality 142
The Subjective Nature of Decisions 143

CHAPTER 32: Notifications to Offerors **145**
Preaward Notification 145
Postaward Notification 146

CHAPTER 33: Debriefings **147**
Preaward Debriefings 147
Postaward Debriefings 148
Responses to Relevant Questions 149
Information That May Not Be Furnished 149
The Manner of Debriefings 150
Preparing for Face-To-Face Debriefings 150
Lessons Learned 150
The End of the Process 151

CHAPTER 34: Task Order Contracts 153
The Source Selection Process for Task Order Contracts 154
Preference for Multiple Awards 154
The Use of Sample Tasks 154
Providing for the Award of Task Orders 155
Awarding Individual Task Orders 155
The Role of the Ombudsman 155
Potential for Streamlining 156

CHAPTER 35: Variations in Source Selection 157
The Advisory Multistep Selection Process 157
Architect-Engineer Services 157
Commercial Item Procurement 159
Streamlined Solicitation for Commercial Items 160
Broad Agency Announcements 160

CHAPTER 36: Ethical Considerations in Source Selection 163
Principles for All Government Employees 163
The Procurement Integrity Act 163
Avoiding the Appearance of Impropriety 164

ACRONYMS AND ABBREVIATIONS 169

GLOSSARY 171

INDEX 187

PREFACE

Although the extent of government reliance on contractors may change over time, it is abundantly clear that the government will always depend on the private sector to provide many goods and services. Quite often government managers must become involved in, or otherwise be affected by, the process used for selecting contractors to supply those goods and services.

Government managers are most effective in the source selection process when they possess a base of knowledge that enables them to influence the process in a positive manner and enables them to judiciously weigh the advice and counsel given to them by other functional area experts.

This book offers government managers the base of source selection knowledge they need. It explains how the source selection process works, it identifies potential impediments, and it guides the manager in making prudent business decisions. And it does so in a logical sequence and without consuming too much of the manager's one irreplaceable resource—time.

To the extent feasible, source selection events are examined in this book in the order in which they are likely to occur. And the pertinent information is presented in succinct single-topic chapters. This permits a manager to focus on any particular part of the process whenever the need for specific information arises.

A glossary is included as a reference, should managers encounter terms with which they are not familiar.

Knowledge of the source selection process is of critical importance to today's government manager. Even the most carefully crafted contract cannot repair the adverse mission impact of making a poor source selection.

—*Chuck Solloway*

Chapter 1

GETTING EVERYONE ON BOARD

Perhaps the most perplexing aspect of the source selection process for a government manager is dealing with the differing perspectives of the various stakeholders. This chapter briefly examines some of these stakeholder issues as well as approaches often used to get everyone on board in formulating a successful source selection strategy.

THE VISION

The Federal Acquisition Regulation (generally known as *the FAR*) describes a vision of the acquisition system in which everyone works together toward a successful outcome; at the same time, it implements myriad laws and policies that can make that goal challenging for the government manager.

Many of these "challenging" FAR requirements and other government acquisition policy mandates can have one or more assigned advocates or proponents within a contracting agency. And each of these advocates is likely to view the source selection process from his or her own unique perspective.

THE STAKEHOLDERS

The primary stakeholders and their likely dominant concerns are as follows:
- The **project or program office** sponsoring an acquisition is committed to an established budget and program schedule. The overriding concern of this stakeholder is to complete the job, achieving satisfactory or better than satisfactory results, within the budget and time allotted. The project or program office is directly accountable to the head of the agency, and perhaps even higher levels of the federal government, to do so.

- The **actual user** of the product or service wants a quality product or service delivered on time. *What* is accomplished is often much more important to this stakeholder than *how* it is accomplished.
- The **contracting officer** must balance the priorities of all of the stakeholders and also seek to avoid contractor protests or other matters that may disrupt or abort the acquisition. The contracting officer and the agency contracting organization must consider a number of discrete goals placed on the agency, such as competition in contracting goals, goals to reduce the use of high cost-risk contract types, and various small business utilization goals. Depending on the current leadership in Congress and the executive department, the emphasis given to any particular goal may vary.

    In addition to complying with regulations and policies, the contracting officer must comply with precedent established by the opinions of the comptroller general or the federal courts in responding to protests from contractors.

    The contracting officer is also expected to perform his or her duties in a manner that is fair to contractors and advantageous to the public.
- The **agency small business advisor** is focused on achieving agency small business goals and on agency compliance with regulations pertaining to the constantly growing number of socioeconomic programs involving small disadvantaged (minority) businesses, veteran-owned businesses, woman-owned businesses, companies in historically underutilized business zones, American Indian-owned businesses, and more. At the least, this stakeholder will insist during the source selection process on compliance with the laws and policies governing socioeconomic programs. These socioeconomic goals, although worthwhile, can add to both the complexity and the cost of the source selection process.
- Each government agency may establish **other special program advocates** for various contract reform efforts such as increasing competition, limiting the use of high-risk contract types, maximizing the use of performance-based requirements documents, and other agency or governmentwide initiatives.
- **Agency legal counsel** seeks to make sure that the agency operates within the law and, in the event of contractor protest or dispute, has a solid, defensible position. Government lawyers tend to practice preventive law and in the main may seem more inclined toward risk avoidance rather than any other aspect of risk management.
- **Representatives from various other agency functional areas** are also involved in the source selection process. These may include safety,

security, quality, or environmental specialists, each with their own set of priorities and concerns.

- **Contractors** are stakeholders, too. They seek business and the opportunity to earn a profit. They want to be treated fairly when they compete for government contracts.

  To the extent that they are permitted do so within law and policy, contractors attempt to influence the decisions of government stakeholders. For example, they may endeavor during the presolicitation stage to impress the program office with their unique capabilities or attempt to influence the program office to favor a particular technical approach. Or they may seek to convince an agency that a socioeconomic set-aside for their particular segment of business is in order.

- The **head of the agency** expects everyone to work together to achieve all agency goals.

- The **source selection authority (SSA)** is the individual who chooses one or more of the competing contractors to receive a contract award. The SSA may rely heavily on the advice and expertise of other stakeholders. The SSA may be the contracting officer or any other designated agency official, such as the project manager or even the agency head.

  The SSA also must approve any source selection strategy developed by the other stakeholders.

Manager Alert

The need for stakeholders to work together in source selection is not just a business management cliché. Any individual stakeholder can be a showstopper in the effort to reach a timely consensus on how to proceed with an acquisition.

COMING TO CONSENSUS ON AN ACQUISITION STRATEGY

There are two basic methods by which agencies seek to bring stakeholders together to develop a consensus on an acquisition strategy. One is for the program or project office to independently develop a strategy and then begin to pass strategy papers back and forth for agreement or comments from a variety of other stakeholders. This process is known as *throwing papers over the wall*. This can be a time-consuming and far less than optimal process, where revised papers repeatedly are thrown back and forth over various functional area walls until the concerns of the various stakeholders are satisfied—or until stakeholders either compromise or surrender their positions.

Another strategy-development method is to hold one or more acquisition strategy meetings where all of the government stakeholders are present. Many agencies require such meetings, especially for big-ticket procurements. The program office, together with the contracting officer, proposes a strategy and gains input from the government stakeholders, all of whom get to both voice their concerns and listen to the concerns of other stakeholders. These strategy meetings should include consideration of any planning input previously provided in planning exchanges with interested contractors.

Typically, these strategy groups are able to reach a consensus. When they do not, agencies normally have a mechanism for obtaining a final strategy decision from higher levels within the agency. These higher-level decisions must also comply with law and regulation.

THE PEOPLE AND THE PROCESS

You cannot separate people from the acquisition process. The astute manager recognizes the legitimate concerns of everyone involved in the source selection process and seeks their assistance. A wagon can be pulled faster and farther when everyone pulls in the same direction.

Chapter 2

AN OVERVIEW OF SOURCE SELECTION

As the term implies, *source selection* denotes the processes by which the government selects a contractor (a source) to furnish goods or services.

SOLE SOURCE VS. COMPETITION

Government acquisition personnel award contracts in one of two ways:
1. They prepare the appropriate justifications, get the required approvals, and award a contract on a noncompetitive basis.
2. They award a contract on the basis of competition.

COMPETITIVE SOURCE SELECTIONS

When award is made on the basis of competition (either full and open competition or limited competition), contractors are normally selected using any one of three selection processes:
1. Award to the responsible, responsive offeror or bidder with the lowest price when only a price has been requested without any other written or oral proposals.
2. Award to the lowest offer among those responsible offerors that, in addition to a price, have submitted a written and/or oral proposal that has been found to be acceptable. This is called the *lowest price, technically acceptable* or *LPTA* process.
3. Award to the responsible contractor offering the best value to the government (which may or may not be the lowest price), considering both price/cost factors and those non-price factors that were identified

in the government solicitation and addressed in the contractor's proposal. This is called the *trade-off* process.

BEST VALUE

Traditionally, the trade-off process was considered to be the only "best value" process. However, the FAR, the acquisition bible of the executive agencies, now defines best value as an *outcome* (rather than a process) that may be achieved by either LPTA or trade-off or some combination of these two processes.

> **Manager Alert**
> To avoid possible misunderstanding, the manager is cautioned that, notwithstanding the current FAR definition, many people in the acquisition community still use *best value* as a synonym for *trade-off* when they communicate with others within and outside the acquisition community. You will also find that *best value* is used as a synonym for *trade-off* in articles published in professional magazines and even in some of the protest opinions issued by the comptroller general or the Court of Federal Claims. This is a longstanding habit that has been hard to break.

FAR SOURCE SELECTION COVERAGE

The coverage of source selection in FAR Part 15 deals *only* with LPTA or trade-off. It is these source selection processes that will be addressed in this book.

PROCESS EVENTS

Exhibit 2-1 is an overview of the activities that take place during the source selection processes. Figures 2-2 and 2-3 are graphic representations of the processes from identification of the government requirement to the point when the source is selected. These representations may include terms and actions not yet familiar to the reader. If that is the case, the meanings will become clear as the reader proceeds through subsequent chapters.

Chapter 2: An Overview of Source Selection

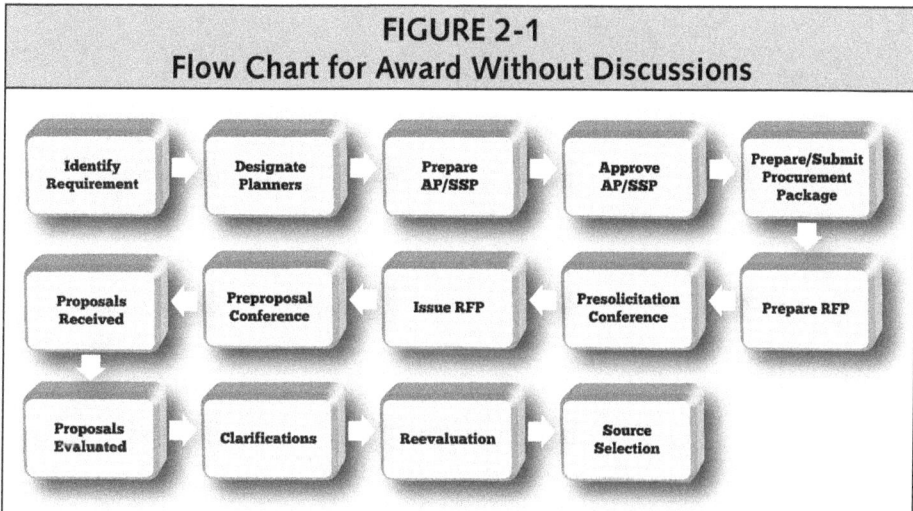

**FIGURE 2-1
Flow Chart for Award Without Discussions**

- Requests for information (RFIs) or draft RFPs may be used at any time prior to RFP preparation.
- Presolicitation conferences may be held prior to or following initial RFP preparation.
- Clarifications are obtained at the discretion of the contracting officer.
- Synopsis at the governmentwide point of entry (GPE) is normally required before issuance of the RFP and following the contract award (source selection).
- Debriefings of competing contractors may be held on a preaward or postaward basis as appropriate.

AP = acquisition plan; SSP = source selection plan; RFP = request for proposal.

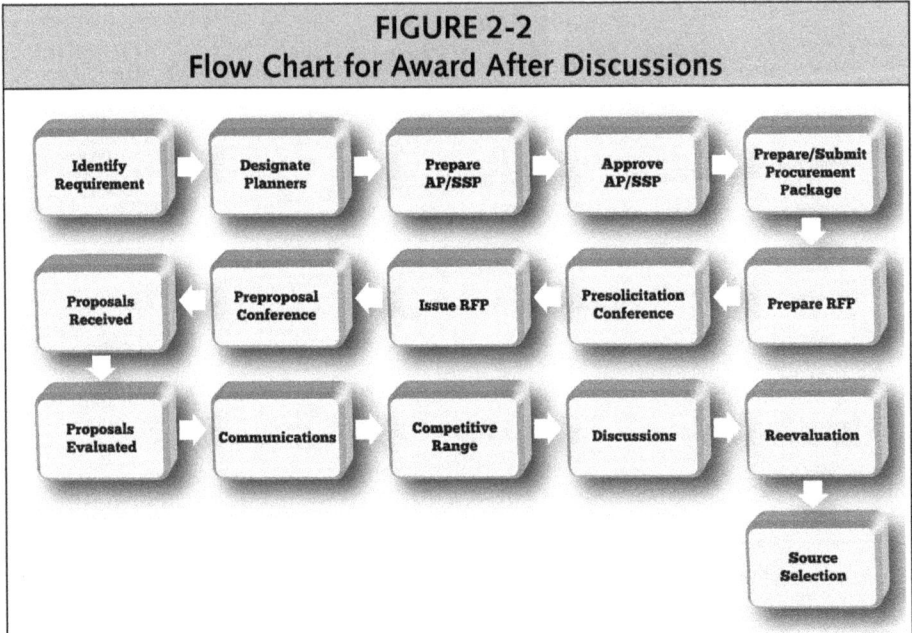

**FIGURE 2-2
Flow Chart for Award After Discussions**

- Requests for information (RFIs) or draft RFPs may be used at any time prior to RFP preparation.
- Presolicitation conferences may be held prior to or following RFP preparation.
- Communications are conducted as needed.
- Synopsis at the governmentwide point of entry (GPE) is normally required before issuance of the RFP and following the contract award (source selection).
- Debriefings of competing contractors may be held on a preaward or postaward basis as appropriate.

AP = acquisition plan; SSP = source selection plan; RFP = request for proposals.

EXHIBIT 2-1
Normal Sequence of Events in Source Selection

When award is to be made without holding discussions with competing contractors

1. Identification of the requirement.
2. Planning begins; assignment of responsibilities.
3. Market research begins.*
4. Preparation of the acquisition plan (AP) and the source selection plan (SSP).
5. Issuance of draft request for proposals (RFP), if any, and other presolicitation exchanges with contractors.**
6. Issuance of a synopsis of the requirement at www.fedbizopps.gov, the governmentwide point of entry (GPE). This notifies the public that a solicitation is to be issued and sometimes occurs while Step 7 is being accomplished.
7. Preparation of the solicitation. An RFP is used for most source selections other than simplified acquisitions. Simplified acquisitions often are accomplished using a request for quotations.
8. Issuance of the solicitation.
9. Preproposal conference and/or site visit, if any.
10. Receipt of proposals.
11. Evaluation of proposals.
12. Obtaining clarifications from offerors, where appropriate.
13. Selecting the source, documenting the rationale, making the award.***
14. Competitors notified; debriefings offered.
15. Debriefings held.

When discussions are to be held with competing contractors

1. Identification of the requirement.
2. Planning begins; assignment of responsibilities.
3. Market research begins.*
4. Preparation of the AP and the SSP.
5. Issuance of draft RFP, if any, and other presolicitation exchanges with contractors.**

6. Issuance of a synopsis of the requirement at www.fedbizopps.gov, the GPE. This notifies the public that a solicitation is to be issued and often occurs while Step 7 is being accomplished.
7. Preparation of the solicitation. An RFP is used for most source selections other than simplified acquisitions. Simplified acquisitions often are accomplished using a request for quotations.
8. Issuance of the solicitation.
9. Preproposal conference or site visit, if any.
10. Receipt of proposals.
11. Evaluation of proposals.
12. Holding of communications, where appropriate.
13. Competitive range established.
14. Those not placed in range notified. Debriefings offered.
15. Debriefings held at time determined by contracting officer (may be delayed until after award at request of competing contractor or determination of the contracting officer).
16. Holding of discussions with those in the competitive range.
17. Interim proposal revisions if permitted or required.
18. Final proposal revisions requested and received.
19. Reevaluation of proposals.
20. Selecting the source, documenting the rationale, making the award.***
21. Competing contractors notified of award and offered debriefing.
22. Debriefings held.

*Steps 3 through 5 may be concurrent.

**Presolicitation exchange opportunities may be synopsized at the GPE.

***Advance notifications before award may be given to competing offerors in the case of set-asides for certain socioeconomic programs.

Chapter 3

LOWEST PRICE, TECHNICALLY ACCEPTABLE VS. TRADE-OFF

Both lowest price, technically acceptable (LPTA) and trade-off source selections require the consideration of at least one other proposal evaluation factor in addition to price or cost and may use any number of these evaluation factors. The non-cost evaluation factors are sometimes referred to as *merit factors* or *technical factors*. Each non-cost evaluation factor, in turn, may have any number of subfactors or may have no subfactors at all.

LOWEST PRICE, TECHNICALLY ACCEPTABLE

In an LPTA selection, offerors must be found acceptable with regard to all cited merit evaluation factors to be considered for award. Award is then made to the acceptable offeror with the lowest price or cost provided that the price or cost has been determined to be fair and reasonable. Some refer to LPTA merit evaluation factors as *go/no go* or *pass/fail factors*. When a source selection is to be made, a competing contractor that remains unacceptable on even a single evaluation factor is not eligible to receive a contract award.

TRADE-OFF

In a trade-off procurement, contractors are scored or rated with regard to the merit factors, which are sometimes called *variable factors*. For example, one or more contractors may be given a rating of "acceptable" while others might be found "outstanding" or even "marginal" or "unacceptable." In trade-off selections, a contract award may be made to a competing contractor offering other than the lowest price or cost, provided that the source selection authority

(SSA) deems the increase in quality, decrease in performance risk, or both to be worth the additional money.

Trade-off procurements are akin to the purchasing we do in our private lives. We look at the differences in quality (as we perceive it) between canned soup options and then decide whether it is worth the extra 30 cents to buy Campbell's soup rather than the store brand.

If a source selection combines both go/no go factors and variable factors, it is considered to be a trade-off source selection. This is so even if only one of several evaluation factors is variable (comparatively scored).

A PRACTICAL EXAMPLE

To demonstrate how these two source selection approaches can result in significantly different outcomes, consider the following hypothetical situation.

A fictional LPTA procurement has three evaluation factors:
1. Contractor technical approach
2. Key personnel
3. Price/cost.

Contractors A, B, and C have all submitted proposals. The offer from A has been judged to be unacceptable. Contractor B has a great technical approach and top-of-the-line personnel. Contractor C has an acceptable but less attractive approach and personnel who just meet government standards. Award will be made without holding discussions.

Prices offered are as follows:
A. $1 million
B. $2 million
C. $1.98 million.

Contractor A cannot get the award because the proposal is not acceptable.

Contractor B cannot get the award because it did not have the lowest price among acceptable proposals.

Contractor C is given the award.

Under LPTA the government must select the lowest price offered among "acceptable" proposals. This is so even where the difference in price is miniscule.

In a trade-off procurement, especially one where the government has made merit factors more important than cost or price, the government could have selected contractor B, which in this case may actually offer the real "best value."

> **Manager Alert**
> In an LPTA procurement, the government must be prepared for a situation where it is compelled to award to the *worst acceptable proposal*.

ADVANTAGES AND DISADVANTAGES OF LPTA

The LPTA method has these advantages and disadvantages:

- Evaluation factors must be established, but they are not assigned relative importance. Each factor is equally as important as any other. This makes preparation of a source selection plan less complex and less time consuming than would be the case if trade-off were used.
- Evaluation of proposals is not normally as difficult as it would be in a trade-off process, since it is not necessary to score or rate competing contractors. Contractors are judged to be either "acceptable" or "not acceptable" on the evaluation factors. Documentation of the bases for these judgments is made a part of the contract file.
- Since award is made to the lowest price or cost among acceptable proposals, the award is relatively easy to document and relatively easy to defend in the event of a contractor protest that challenges the choice made by the government.
- The strong emphasis on low cost or price is believed to encourage competing contractors to "sharpen their pencils" and may well result in prices that are lower than would have been obtained if the trade-off process had been used.
- Of the two source selection processes, LPTA is usually less labor intensive for the government and usually takes less time.
- The government may have to select less than the true best value when LPTA is used. In fact, as stated previously, the government may have to select the worst acceptable proposal.

Considering all the advantages to the government, including lower administrative cost and less consumption of time, government planners can reasonably conclude that using LPTA will result in the overall best value to the government for a specific procurement. This may be especially so when acquisition planners anticipate that there will be minimal quality or risk discriminators between likely competitors.

ADVANTAGES AND DISADVANTAGES OF TRADE-OFF

The trade-off method has these advantages and disadvantages:

- Evaluation factors must be established, and the relative importance of those factors must be determined. This normally consumes more planning time than the LPTA process. Factor selection and weighting must be carefully done because the government will ultimately have to make business judgments that are "not inconsistent" with the proposal evaluation factors and their relative importance, as set forth in the government solicitation.
- Proposal evaluators must score or rate each competing contractor on each evaluation factor and prepare supporting rationale. Again, this is more labor intensive than LPTA.
- Trade-off is a relatively subjective process wherein the SSA is given great latitude in choosing a contractor. He or she is expected to exercise good business judgment and to clearly and persuasively document the rationale for award. The SSA thus must assume a great deal of responsibility. The law provides only that he or she is required to make a rational decision that is consistent with the evaluation scheme set forth in the request for proposals.
- Because individual business judgment is exercised in the award, and because the evaluation process is more complex, there is more opportunity for error, disagreement, and contractor protest when using trade-off.
- The trade-off process almost always takes more time than an LPTA selection.
- Trade-off increases the likelihood of obtaining the true best value among competing proposals since it gives the government (the appointed SSA) far more flexibility in applying business judgment.

Notwithstanding any disadvantages inherent in the trade-off process, acquisition officials may reasonably conclude that for a particular procurement, the amount of money involved, the inherent contract performance risk, and/or its criticality warrants using this traditional method of obtaining best value. Trade-off permits the application of reasoned business judgment, rather than selecting a winning contractor by calculator.

AGENCY GUIDANCE

Some published agency guidance may encourage or require the use of one or the other of these processes for particular categories of procurements. For example, agencies often strongly encourage the use of the trade-off process in research and development procurements and in major systems acquisitions.

Chapter 4

THE ACQUISITION PLAN AND THE SOURCE SELECTION PLAN

FAR Part 7 requires that planning take place for all procurements and gives a format for written acquisition plans. Agency regulations, in turn, identify the dollar amount and character of those procurements that will require a written acquisition plan. For example, an agency may require written plans for all procurements in excess of $1 million as well as for any other procurements that the head of the agency (or a designee) determines to be significant enough to require a written plan. Another agency may establish only $100,000 as the dollar threshold for requiring a written plan.

The FAR also requires that the head of the agency (or a designee) designate planners for an acquisition. As a practical matter, acquisition planning usually begins with an assigned program official who must—in view of the many matters that must be addressed—quickly enlist the services of a contracting officer.

THE ACQUISITION PLAN

The format prescribed in FAR 7.105 for a written acquisition plan requires that a significant number of issues be addressed. According to FAR guidelines, one part of the plan must be devoted specifically to source selection procedures. Other parts of the plan, such as the treatment of contract cost and the consideration of streamlining techniques, also directly impact how the source selection is to be conducted. An outline of the acquisition plan format is shown in Exhibit 4-1.

THE ACQUISITION TEAM

Planning for an acquisition is the joint responsibility of all members of the acquisition team and should begin as soon as a requirement (need) is identified. FAR 1.102(c) defines the acquisition team as consisting of "all participants in Government acquisition including not only representatives of the technical, supply, and procurement communities but also the customers they serve, and the contractors who provide the products and services." In some agencies, the multidisciplinary team that is established to guide a requirement through the source selection process is known as an integrated product team.

Of particular note in the above FAR quote is the inclusion of contractors as a part of the team. It recognizes that to be a smart buyer, the government should have input from the private sector.

The FAR also makes it abundantly clear that contractor participation should not be limited to just proposal preparation and any subsequent contract performance. In FAR Part 15, which deals principally with lowest price, technically acceptable (LPTA) and trade-off acquisition, officials are encouraged to "exchange information among all interested parties from the identification of a requirement." Those "interested parties" include potential offerors (contractors), government contracting and program personnel, and end users.

FAR Part 1 goes on to state that the role of each acquisition team member is to exercise "personal initiative" and "sound business judgment" in providing the best value to the customer. It further makes it clear that these acquisition planners have a great deal of discretion, as it provides that any acquisition strategy that is not otherwise prohibited by law (including case law), regulation, or executive order is a permissible exercise of authority. Thus the FAR encourages the use of creative acquisition techniques, including techniques designed to streamline the acquisition process.

THE SOURCE SELECTION STRATEGY

Both FAR and individual agency regulations require that acquisition planning address the source selection strategy. Often this strategy is reflected in a separate document known as the source selection plan (SSP). An SSP may be referenced in, repeated in, or attached to the acquisition plan. See Exhibit 4-2 for one agency's version of the SSP.

THE CONTENTS OF A SOURCE SELECTION PLAN

Typically, an SSP addresses such matters as:
- Assignment of the source selection authority

- The process to be used—LPTA or trade-off
- Evaluation factors and any significant subfactors
- The relative importance of the factors and subfactors (for trade-off)
- Socioeconomic considerations, such as the use of small businesses, small disadvantaged businesses, woman-owned businesses, and others
- The source selection organization and the persons or types of persons to be used as evaluators or advisors
- The information that will be required in proposals and the manner in which the information is to be conveyed
- Any special considerations, such as the use of multiphase selection or streamlining techniques, licenses required, or coordination required with other agencies
- Schedules and milestones
- Forms to be used, such as evaluation forms and nondisclosure forms.

Each agency establishes responsibility for preparing the plan and establishes plan approval levels.

FORMATS OF THE ACQUISITION PLAN AND SOURCE SELECTION PLANS

As may be seen in Exhibits 4-1 and 4-2, the written acquisition plan prescribed by FAR Part 7 includes information that is required in an SSP plus a great deal more.

> **Manager Alert**
>
> In many agencies, various levels are established for review and approval of both acquisition plans and source selection plans. In some cases, obtaining those reviews and approvals can be a tedious, bureaucratic process. Thus, there is a tendency to treat an approved plan as if it were written in stone. However, as time progresses, government planners typically learn more and more about market conditions, the state of the art, and individual contractor capabilities that are relevant to a particular acquisition. If there is a benefit to be derived from changing a plan, then it should be changed. Sticking with a game plan that called for long passes doesn't make much sense when a dense fog has settled over the playing field.

> **EXHIBIT 4-1**
> **Outline of the Contents of a Written Acquisition Plan (FAR Part 7)**
>
> (a) Acquisition background and objectives
>   1. Statement of need
>   2. Applicable conditions
>   3. Cost
>   (i) Life-cycle cost
>   (ii) Design-to cost
>   (iii) Application of should-cost
>   4. Capability or performance
>   5. Delivery or performance period requirements
>   6. Trade-offs
>   7. Risks
>   8. Acquisition streamlining
> (b) Plan of action
>   1. Sources
>   2. Competition
>   3. Source selection procedures
>   4. Acquisition considerations
>   5. Budgeting and funding
>   6. Product or service description
>   7. Priorities, allocations, and allotments
>   8. Contractor vs. government performance
>   9. Inherently governmental functions
>   10. Management information requirements
>   11. Make or buy
>   12. Test and evaluation
>   13. Logistics considerations
>   14. Government-furnished property
>   15. Government-furnished information
>   16. Environmental and energy conservation objectives
>   17. Security considerations
>   18. Contract administration
>   19. Other considerations
>   20. Milestones for the acquisition cycle
>   - Additional requirements for major systems
>   - Additional requirements for acquisitions involving bundling
>   - Additional requirements for telecommuting

EXHIBIT 4-2
Sample Best Value (Trade-off) Source Selection Plan

Section I: Overview

A. Description of requirement
B. Acquisition approach

Section II: Solicitation provisions

A. Basis for award
B. Factors and subfactors to be evaluated
    1. Factor I: Technical
    2. Factor II: Past performance
    3. Factor III: Small business participation plan
    4. Factor IV: Cost or price
C. Evaluation approach
    1. Technical evaluation approach
        a. Understanding of the requirement
        b. Feasibility of approach
        c. Flexibility
    2. Past performance evaluation approach
    3. Price/cost evaluation approach
D. Proposal submission
    1. Format
    2. File packaging
    3. Page count
    4. Content requirements
        a. Volume I: Technical approach
        b. Volume II: Past performance
            (1) Section 1: Contract descriptions
            (2) Section 2: Performance
            (3) Section 3: New corporate entities
            (4) Section 4: Past performance questionnaire
        c. Volume III: Small business participation plan
        d. Volume IV: Price/cost
        e. Volume V: Solicitation, offer, and award documents and certifications/representations

Section III: Evaluation organization and responsibilities
A. Evaluation organizations
    1. SSA
    2. SSAC (optional)
    3. SSEB
    4. PCO
B. Responsibilities of the organizational elements
    1. SSA
    2. SSAC
    3. SSEB
    4. PCO
C. Composition of the organizational elements

Section IV: Evaluation procedures
A. Agenda
B. Definitions
C. Rating method
D. Proposal evaluation
E. Source selection
F. Announcement of selection
G. Debriefing of unsuccessful offerors

Section V: Policies, instructions, and standards of conduct
A. General
B. Safeguarding procurement information
C. Evaluation procedures

Appendices
A. Members of and advisors to the source selection evaluation board
B. Source selection participation agreement
C. Summary evaluation form
D. Item for negotiation form
E. Item for negotiation evaluation form

Attachments

Past performance questionnaire

Source: Department of the Army Contracting Center for Excellence, undated document.

SSA = source selection authority; SSAC = source selection advisory council; SSEB = source selection evaluation board; PCO = procuring contracting officer/principal contracting officer.

Chapter 5

PROTESTS

Contractor protests may occur at any time during source selection. For this reason, and because protests will be referred to in later chapters, the subject is being addressed early in this book.

EXTRAORDINARY CONTRACTOR RIGHTS

Among the extraordinary rights of the sellers in government contracting is a contractor's right to protest the actions of the government in the source selection process. As you will see, this can sometimes result in great delay and expense to the government.

THE STAY PROVISIONS

The Competition in Contracting Act (CICA) generally requires that any award be delayed until the protest is resolved whenever a protest is filed with the Government Accountability Office (GAO) prior to award of a contract. If award has already been made and a timely protest is lodged, then some sort of stop work order is issued until some resolution is reached. These provisions of CICA are known as the *stay provisions* or *stay rules*. The FAR invokes similar stay rules for protests made to the procuring agency.

OVERRIDE PROCEDURES

If an offeror has submitted a timely protest to the GAO in order to get a protest opinion from the head of the GAO, called the comptroller general (informally, "Comp Gen"), the government may proceed with award (or continue performance if contract award has already been made) only in cases of documented urgency and approval of the head of the contracting activity. Some other designated approval level is required if the protest has been submitted only to the agency.

For most protests, a documentation of urgency is not developed approval is not sought and the stay provisions prevail. If a government agency does, however, decide to use the urgency override procedure, the protester has the right to challenge the override in the Court of Federal Claims.

DEFINITION OF A PROTEST

FAR 33.101 defines a protest as a written objection by an interested party to any of the following:
- A solicitation or other request by an agency for offers for a contract for the procurement of property or services
- Cancellation of the solicitation or other request
- Award or proposed award of a contract
- A termination or cancellation of an award of a contract when it is alleged that the termination or cancellation is based in whole or part on improprieties concerning the award of the contract.

There are two basic types of protests:
1. A preaward protest made before a contract is awarded
2. A postaward protest made after a contract has been awarded.

The protest coverage in FAR Part 33 is extensive and includes instructions to contractors for submitting protests and guidance for the government on handling protests.

WHAT IS AN INTERESTED PARTY?

An *interested party* is an actual or prospective offeror whose direct economic interest would be affected by award of a contract or failure to award a contract. When a competing contractor protests, the protestor must show that, except for the agency's actions, it would have had a substantial chance to receive the award. If that is not the case, no harm was done to the protester as a result of government action, and the comptroller general will normally not address the issue raised in the protest. This has been characterized by some in the business as the "no harm, no foul" rule.

An interested party may file a protest with
- The agency conducting the acquisition
- The GAO (comptroller general)
- The Court of Federal Claims.

Because of time limitations, expense, and other considerations, the overwhelming majority of protests are filed with the agency or with the GAO.

MATTERS ADDRESSED IN PROTESTS

Preaward protests may challenge solicitation provisions (including evaluation factors or their relative importance), any government-imposed limitations on competition, or any other matters where an offeror believes that the government is acting in violation of law, regulation, or basic issues of fairness.

Postaward protests often address alleged erroneous or biased proposal evaluations, government failure to act in accordance with the provisions of the solicitation, government failure to hold meaningful discussions, unequal treatment of offerors, and other such matters.

TIMELINESS

In addition to meeting the interested party criteria, protests generally must be filed before the closing date established for receipt of proposals if a protest concerning solicitation provisions is to be considered. If a postaward protest is to be made, then the protest should be filed within ten days of the time the protested issue was known or should have been known. For example, if the issue is not discovered until a debriefing, then the contractor has ten days from the debriefing to file a protest. However, to invoke the CICA stay provisions, a competing contractor must file a protest that is based on information discovered at a debriefing within five days after the debriefing was held or was offered to be held.

WHEN INTERESTED PARTY OR TIMELINESS STANDARDS ARE NOT MET

If a protester does not meet either or both of the interested party and timely submission criteria, it is likely that the issue being protested will not be considered. However, although relatively rare, occasions do arise when the comptroller general will consider and publish an opinion on the merits of protests that did not meet these standards. In the past these occasions have been limited to instances where the comptroller general felt that the issue involved was "significant to the procurement system" or was "of widespread interest to the procurement community" or both. In other words, the comptroller general felt that it would benefit the acquisition process if case law (i.e., precedent) were to be established for the issue or issues involved.

COMPTROLLER GENERAL DECISION TIMES

The comptroller general normally has 100 days from the date a protest was filed to issue a decision. If the protestor elects, an expedited consideration of the issue may be made under an express option. A decision is normally issued under this option within 65 days.

AGENCY RESPONSIBILITIES

The FAR suggests that agencies avoid protests by making their best efforts to resolve concerns raised by an interested party at the contracting officer level through open and frank discussions. Protests are expensive and time consuming, and they can have significant adverse impact on the orderly progression of government programs. Obviously, every reasonable effort should be made to avoid their occurrence.

FAR 33.103 advises that, if a protest is made to the agency, the agency "should provide for inexpensive, informal, procedurally simple, and expeditious resolution of protests." And it advises that alternative dispute resolution (ADR) techniques, involvement of neutral third parties, and use of another agency's personnel may be appropriate. Many agencies have adopted and successfully used ADR procedures for protests.

IMPACT OF PROTESTS

To understand the impact protests can have on government operations, consider the following actual sequence of events involving a solicitation for proposals to operate a publications clearinghouse:

1. The source selection was to be based on technical acceptability, past performance, and cost.
2. Two of the contenders for this competitive small business set-aside were firms named Logistics Applications Inc. (LAI) and Biospherics Incorporated.
3. A review panel reviewed each proposal for acceptability. LAI was found technically unacceptable, and Biospherics was awarded the contract.
4. LAI protested that the review panel was likely biased since two of the six members of the panel were former employees of Biospherics.
5. The agency convened a new panel and, since corrective action had been taken, the comptroller general dismissed the LAI protest as academic.
6. The new panel considered both firms to be acceptable, and both were included in the competitive range.
7. Discussions were held and final revised proposals were received.

8. LAI was given the award.
9. Biospherics then submitted a protest to the GAO contending that its proposal should have been found technically superior.
10. In reviewing the agency documentation, the comptroller general found that "the record is devoid of any documentation of the agency's evaluation of final revised proposals. . . . In the absence of such documentation, we are unable to determine the reasonableness of the agency's evaluation upon which the selection of LAI for award was made."
11. The comptroller general made the following recommendations:
    a. Reevaluation of proposals and a new selection decision.
    b. If after reevaluation the agency believes further discussions are warranted, it may reopen discussions and request another round of revised proposals.
    c. If the agency determines that LAI is no longer in line for award, the agency should terminate the award to LAI and make another award.
    d. Biospherics should be reimbursed for its cost of filing and pursuing the protest, including reasonable attorneys' fees.

At the time the comptroller general opinion was issued, 480 days had already elapsed since the solicitation was first issued, and the source selection process was still far from complete. In addition to the delays, the government had incurred significant expenses, including costs associated with defending against the protest, costs that were reimbursed to the protester, and, potentially, costs associated with contract termination.

Unfortunately, this is not a worst-case scenario. There have been many sustained protests where delay and monetary consequences were far more severe. We chose this example because, in retrospect, it appears that the issues involved were clear-cut and the problems probably could have been avoided.

ATTORNEY FEES AND BID AND PROPOSAL COSTS

Government payment of protestor attorney fees and government payment of protestor bid and proposal costs are often in order. In some cases, these are substantial. For example, in Alabama Aircraft Industries Inc.-Birmingham, No. 08-470C, reissued February 3, 2009, the Court of Federal Claims found that the protestor was entitled to $1,003,288.23 in bid and proposal costs. And the comptroller general found that attorney fees of $475.00 per hour (for 324.15 hours) were reasonable in CourtSmart Digital Systems Inc., B-292995.7, March 18, 2005.

> **Manager Alert**
>
> Obviously, a government agency should strive to avoid receiving a protest whenever it can. And it should strive to avoid a successful protest if, despite its efforts to prevent it, a protest is filed. Knowledge of the regulations, laws, and issues involved in source selection can help agencies avoid protests or minimize the likelihood of successful protests.

Chapter 6

ORGANIZING FOR SOURCE SELECTION

In any source selection, there must be a source selection authority (SSA), a contracting officer, and one or more evaluators. Sometimes a single person can perform more than one of these roles.

THE SOURCE SELECTION AUTHORITY

The SSA is an individual appointed by the agency head to—among other assigned responsibilities—select the source at the end of the source selection process. If no one else is appointed, then the contracting officer is the SSA. Thus, to use a computing term, the contracting officer is the default SSA.

Who, other than the contracting officer, can be appointed as SSA? There are no governmentwide restrictions absent some sort of conflict of interest. Usually, the more significant the procurement, the higher on the organization chart agencies will go to appoint an SSA.

DUTIES OF THE SOURCE SELECTION AUTHORITY

The SSA must be identified very early in the acquisition cycle in view of the mandatory duties FAR 15.303(b) gives this individual. The FAR provides that the SSA *shall*

- Establish an evaluation team tailored for the particular acquisition
- Approve the source selection strategy or acquisition plan
- Ensure consistency among the various solicitation provisions
- Consider the recommendations of advisory boards or panels (if any)
- Select the source that will provide the best value.

THE ROLE OF THE CONTRACTING OFFICER

Typically, for more routine source selections, the contracting officer is the SSA. He or she will normally have a small group of evaluators to review and evaluate the technical (non-cost) aspects of proposals and one or more assigned persons to perform a cost or price analysis.

Even when the contracting officer is not the SSA, he or she has a key role in the selection process as an advisor to the SSA and others involved in the source selection process.

After release of the solicitation, the contracting officer is always the individual who controls any oral or written contacts with competing contractors.

EVALUATORS

The name given the group of non-cost-factor evaluators differs from agency to agency and sometimes even within agencies. Some of the more common names are

- Technical evaluation panel
- Technical evaluation team
- Proposal evaluation board
- Source selection evaluation board.

FORMAL AND OTHER THAN FORMAL SOURCE SELECTION

Governmentwide regulations at one time distinguished between "formal" source selections and "other than formal" source selections. "Although" this is no longer the case, some individual agency regulations still make this distinction. And some even refer to "other than formal" source selections as *informal*, an unfortunate choice of a name for a disciplined process.

More formal source selections (i.e., those source selections with a higher dollar value or those otherwise determined to be of particular significance) have more complicated organization structures than merely a small group of evaluators. Figure 6-1 shows an example of one such structure.

Chapter 6

ORGANIZING FOR SOURCE SELECTION

In any source selection, there must be a source selection authority (SSA), a contracting officer, and one or more evaluators. Sometimes a single person can perform more than one of these roles.

THE SOURCE SELECTION AUTHORITY

The SSA is an individual appointed by the agency head to—among other assigned responsibilities—select the source at the end of the source selection process. If no one else is appointed, then the contracting officer is the SSA. Thus, to use a computing term, the contracting officer is the default SSA.

Who, other than the contracting officer, can be appointed as SSA? There are no governmentwide restrictions absent some sort of conflict of interest. Usually, the more significant the procurement, the higher on the organization chart agencies will go to appoint an SSA.

DUTIES OF THE SOURCE SELECTION AUTHORITY

The SSA must be identified very early in the acquisition cycle in view of the mandatory duties FAR 15.303(b) gives this individual. The FAR provides that the SSA *shall*

- Establish an evaluation team tailored for the particular acquisition
- Approve the source selection strategy or acquisition plan
- Ensure consistency among the various solicitation provisions
- Consider the recommendations of advisory boards or panels (if any)
- Select the source that will provide the best value.

THE ROLE OF THE CONTRACTING OFFICER

Typically, for more routine source selections, the contracting officer is the SSA. He or she will normally have a small group of evaluators to review and evaluate the technical (non-cost) aspects of proposals and one or more assigned persons to perform a cost or price analysis.

Even when the contracting officer is not the SSA, he or she has a key role in the selection process as an advisor to the SSA and others involved in the source selection process.

After release of the solicitation, the contracting officer is always the individual who controls any oral or written contacts with competing contractors.

EVALUATORS

The name given the group of non-cost-factor evaluators differs from agency to agency and sometimes even within agencies. Some of the more common names are

- Technical evaluation panel
- Technical evaluation team
- Proposal evaluation board
- Source selection evaluation board.

FORMAL AND OTHER THAN FORMAL SOURCE SELECTION

Governmentwide regulations at one time distinguished between "formal" source selections and "other than formal" source selections. "Although" this is no longer the case, some individual agency regulations still make this distinction. And some even refer to "other than formal" source selections as *informal*, an unfortunate choice of a name for a disciplined process.

More formal source selections (i.e., those source selections with a higher dollar value or those otherwise determined to be of particular significance) have more complicated organization structures than merely a small group of evaluators. Figure 6-1 shows an example of one such structure.

Chapter 6: Organizing for Source Selection 29

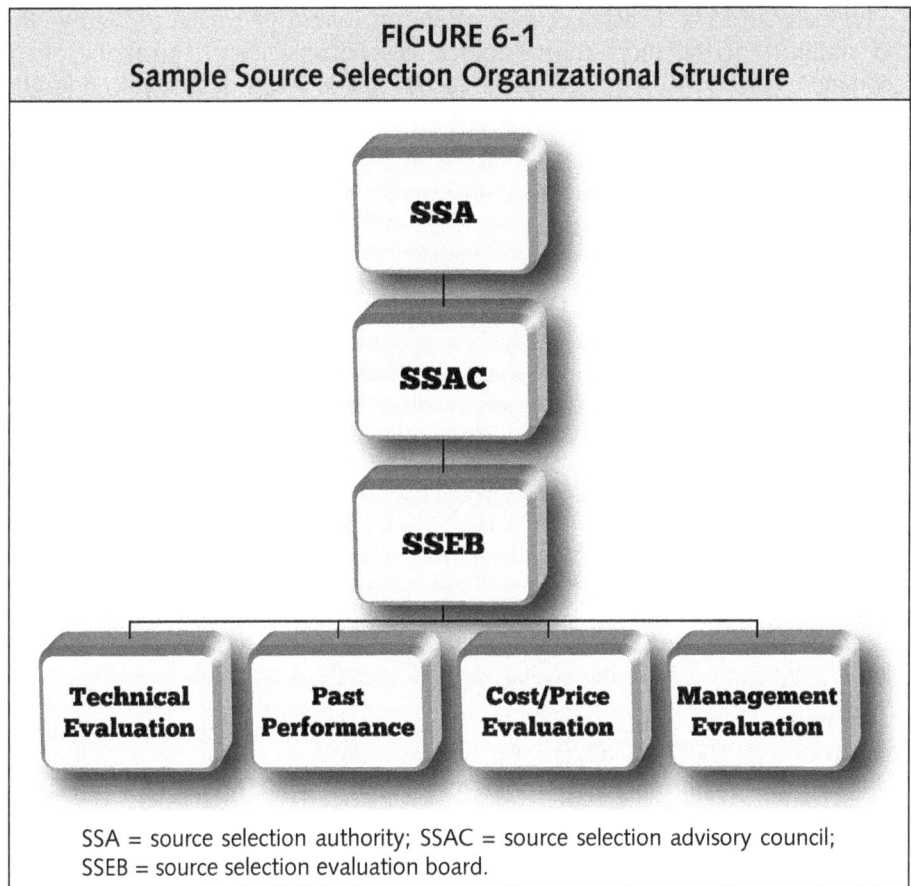

FIGURE 6-1
Sample Source Selection Organizational Structure

SSA = source selection authority; SSAC = source selection advisory council; SSEB = source selection evaluation board.

In some agencies, a separate group of individuals is responsible solely for past performance evaluation. Sometimes this group is known as a performance risk assessment group.

ADVISORS

The duties of the source selection advisory council (SSAC) shown in Figure 6-1 (or an equivalent group in other agency organizational structures) normally include overseeing the operations of the source selection evaluation board and advising the SSA. This advice to the SSA may or may not include a recommendation for award (selection), depending on agency regulations, standard agency practices, or the wishes of the SSA.

Typically, an SSAC consists of military and/or civilian personnel of high grade and stature. For the more formal source selections, agency regulations often recommend that SSAC members be at specific grade levels depending upon the nature and dollar value of the particular acquisition.

In addition to the SSAC or its equivalent, the SSA may have a number of other advisors, including a business advisor (often the contracting officer), a small business advisor, legal counsel, and others.

THE NUMBER OF EVALUATORS AND ADVISORS

Evaluators for any given source selection can range in number from one person to more than 100. In fact, some source selection organizational structures have had as many as 200 people assigned as evaluators and advisors.

There is no evidence available that links the number of people involved in proposal evaluation with the wisdom of a source selection decision. In fact, some suspect that the use of very large numbers of evaluators and advisors can contribute to communication static and to miscommunication between subject matter experts and the SSA. Nonetheless, no matter how large or small the crowd, it is important that proposal evaluators as an entity have the full range of expertise needed to competently address all of the evaluation factors in the solicitation.

For more routine source selections, most agencies have, either by longstanding practice or regulation, established a minimum number of evaluators. Usually this is an odd number (three, five, or seven, for example), which presumably facilitates voting in the event of disagreement.

THE ORIGIN OF EVALUATORS AND ADVISORS

Technical evaluators, cost evaluators, and advisors are chosen because of their expertise. Most are employees of the procuring agency, but persons from other government agencies may be used when appropriate, such as when sufficient expertise is not available in-house, when the agency wants to protect itself from charges of organizational bias, or when other agencies will be the users of the product or service being procured.

Involving the users in the source selection process may later reduce the number of complaints about business decisions made during the source selection process.

USE OF CONTRACTORS AS EVALUATORS AND ADVISORS

Contractor personnel may also be used as evaluators or advisors. Office of Management and Budget (OMB) guidelines, as described in FAR Subpart 7.5, provide that contractors may participate as "technical advisors to a source selection board" or may participate as "voting or non-voting members of a source evaluation board." However, common sense tells us that acquisition planners should work closely with legal counsel when considering the use of contractor personnel as advisors or evaluators. Planners and legal counsel should thoroughly address issues such as conflicts of interest and protection of source selection and proprietary information.

> **Manager Alert**
> The OMB provisions described in the FAR also state that a contractor may *not* participate as "a voting member on any source selection board." This is usually not a problem because the FAR requires that source selections be made by an individual rather than a board.

COMPETENCE AND FAIRNESS

Competing contractors have on occasion based protests on the perceived lack of expertise of evaluators or on allegations of evaluator bias. These are rarely successful because protesting contractors have to *show* incompetence or bias, not just proclaim it. For example, they must show how and where the alleged bias occurred, or how and where the alleged incompetence manifested itself in a way that prejudiced the protestor. Typical of comptroller general opinions on this matter is the following excerpt from a January 2008 opinion:

> We have long found that the selection of evaluators is a matter within the discretion of the agency, and, accordingly, we do not review allegations . . . concerning the evaluators' qualifications or the composition of evaluation panels absent a showing of possible fraud, conflict of interest, or actual bias on the part of evaluation officials (IMLCORP LLC; Wattre Corp., B-310582 et al., January 9, 2008).

This is not to say that there have not been some successful protests based on allegations of bias or incompetence. In one instance, an offeror's proposal in a competition that could have resulted in "outsourcing" of work that was being done by government personnel was found by government evaluators to be unacceptable. However, the offeror pointed out that a number of the evaluators who had found the proposal to be unacceptable stood to lose their jobs if the proposal had been found to be acceptable. The potential for bias was obviously so great that the agency determined that a new evaluation by other evaluators was necessary.

Agencies should take evaluator competency and potential conflicts of interest seriously.

When functional supervisors are asked to furnish someone to be an evaluator for an acquisition, they may be tempted to designate the person they can most afford to do without during the source selection process. Source selection authorities and contracting officers should always insist on highly qualified personnel, not just as protection against a protest, but to maximize the chances that the real best value is identified and chosen.

SOURCE SELECTION RULES

Regardless of the size and structure of the organization established for the source selection, and regardless of the grade levels of those involved, the source selection rules and the source selection issues described in this book remain the same.

Chapter 7

MARKET RESEARCH

Conducting market research, as addressed in FAR Part 10, is required by law. While the FAR addresses both the goals of market research and, to some extent, the manner in which it can be conducted, it does not specify the amount of time and money that can or should be spent on market research. Instead, the FAR leaves this to the business judgment of agency officials, based on the size, scope, criticality, and complexity of the acquisition. For example, it might be overkill to spend $200,000 on market research for a relatively straightforward acquisition of modest value, but an expenditure of that size may not be enough for a specific complex, multimillion-dollar acquisition.

REQUIREMENTS AND GOALS

Market research is required whenever

- A new requirements document is being generated
- Offers are to be solicited for acquisitions with an estimated value in excess of the simplified acquisition threshold
- Offers are to be solicited for acquisitions of a lesser value when circumstances justify the cost of market research
- Offers are to be solicited for acquisitions that could lead to a *bundled contract*—a contract for combined requirements that had previously been procured separately.

One of the major goals of market research is to determine if commercial items, modified commercial items, or nondevelopmental items (NDI) are available to meet government needs either totally or at component levels. Other goals are to identify industry practices in the commercial marketplace (when applicable), to ensure maximum use of recovered materials and promote energy conservation and efficiency, to determine whether bundling (combining requirements) would be appropriate, and to assess the availability of technology that meets applicable accessibility standards issued by the Architectural and Transportation Barriers Compliance Board.

THE SMART BUYER CONCEPT

Clearly, market research is intended to make the government a "smart buyer" through identifying what is actually available to meet government needs before the agency attempts to buy it. Identifying commercial items and NDIs can help the government avoid the expense of reinventing the wheel.

Market research efforts should also include consideration of socioeconomic issues, the availability of competition, and possible cost/quality/performance trade-offs when finalizing government requirements.

MARKET RESEARCH TECHNIQUES

FAR 10.002 identifies the following techniques for conducting market research:
- Contacting knowledgeable individuals in government or industry
- Reviewing the results of previous market research for the same or similar requirements
- Publishing formal requests for information in technical, scientific, or business publications
- Querying governmentwide databases to identify procurement instruments intended for use by multiple agencies (such as many task order contracts maintained by the General Services Administration)
- Participating in interactive online communications with industry, acquisition personnel, and customers
- Obtaining source lists for similar requirements from government or industry sources
- Reviewing product literature, either printed or online
- Conducting interchange meetings or holding presolicitation conferences to involve potential offerors early in the acquisition process.

> **Manager Alert**
> Since FAR Part 10 indicates that market research should be conducted on "an ongoing basis," and since this guidance clearly applies to both the program and contracting communities, program personnel should work closely with the contracting officer to avoid inadvertently releasing protected procurement information whenever a solicitation has been issued or is about to be issued.

DOCUMENTATION OF MARKET RESEARCH

FAR 10.002(e) requires that agencies document the results of market research in an appropriate manner. Agency regulations may require or suggest a particular format.

Chapter 8

INVOLVING CONTRACTORS IN SOURCE SELECTION PLANNING

The FAR calls any dialogue (written or oral) between the government and any contractors who are competing for or may be competing for a specific contract an *exchange*. Within FAR-restricted limits, exchanges may take place before a solicitation (i.e., a request for proposal or RFP) is issued or at various times following the issuance of a solicitation.

CONTRACTOR PARTICIPATION ENCOURAGED

FAR 15.201 specifically encourages "exchanges with industry before receipt of proposals." When these exchanges are conducted prior to issuance of a solicitation, they are known as *presolicitation exchanges*.

PRESOLICITATION EXCHANGES: ISSUES AND TECHNIQUES

According to FAR 15.201, presolicitation exchanges involving contractors may address "concerns" involving

- The acquisition strategy, including the proposed contract type, terms and conditions, and planning schedules
- The feasibility of the requirement, including performance requirements, statements of work, and data requirements
- The suitability of contemplated proposal preparation instructions

- Evaluation criteria
- The approach planned for assessing past performance information
- Any other industry concerns or questions.

The techniques identified for conducting presolicitation exchanges include the following:
- Industry or small business conferences
- Public hearings
- Market research
- One-on-one meetings
- Draft requests for proposals
- Requests for information
- Presolicitation conferences
- Where appropriate, site visits.

Conferences and Public Hearings

Agencies regularly hold conferences and hearings to notify industry of current and planned government acquisitions. These events are most fruitful when potential contractors are given opportunities to voice opinions and to ask or answer questions on a one-on-one basis. Contractors are often reluctant to bring some issues up in open forums in front of competitors.

Draft Requests for Proposals

Draft RFPs allow contractors to consider in depth what the government is contemplating putting in the final RFP and gives those contractors an opportunity to make potentially valuable observations and suggestions. Thus, draft RFPs are most valuable to government planners when they include material such as the proposed statement of work, the proposed proposal preparation instructions, the proposed evaluation factors (and, when appropriate, the relative importance of those factors), proposed data requirements, and the like.

The challenge for government planners is, of course, to determine which of the comments received from potential contractors are meaningful and which are merely self-serving. Separating the wheat from the chaff is essential.

Requests for Information

Requests for information are normally prepared using an agency-prescribed format and usually include a disclaimer that the government will not be obligated in any way by contractor participation.

One-on-One Meetings with Potential Sources

The FAR now seems to grant a great deal more latitude regarding one-on-one meetings than it has in the past. It permits one-on-one discussions regarding any or all of the concerns mentioned previously, including the feasibility of the requirement, proposal preparation instructions, and evaluation criteria.

The FAR states that one-on-one preproposal meetings (which include any presolicitation meetings) that are "substantially involved with contract terms and conditions should involve the contracting officer." There are two potentially significant issues here. One concerns the phrase "contract terms and conditions." Presumably, this excludes matters that apply only to the solicitation, such as proposal preparation instructions and proposal evaluation criteria. The other significant issue is use of the word *should*. In FAR parlance, *should* normally means that something ought to be done, but it is not mandatory. When the FAR intends to make something mandatory, the word *shall* or *must* is used.

This FAR coverage can be interpreted only as an effort to give program personnel more flexibility in acquisition planning, including source selection planning, and to help make sure they have done all of their homework before committing the government to a strategy.

Limits on One-on-One Meetings

FAR 15.201 does place some limits on one-on-one meetings:

> When specific information about a proposed acquisition that would be necessary for the preparation of proposals is disclosed to one or more potential offerors, the information must be made available to the public as soon as practicable but no later than the next general release of information, in order to avoid creating an unfair competitive advantage.

This requires the exercise of good judgment, since the FAR has not placed any specific time limits on the "next general release of information." Is it too long a time, for example, if the next general release will be six months after the one-on-one, when the proposed acquisition is to be advertised at the governmentwide point of entry? Until the FAR language is made more specific, or this issue is brought before the comptroller general or the courts, reasonable application of the guidance would be in order to avoid giving one or more contractors an "unfair competitive advantage."

While one-on-one meetings "should" under certain circumstances involve the contracting officer, any meeting held after issuance of the solicitation (RFP) *must* involve the contracting officer. FAR Part 15 requires that the contracting officer be the focal point of exchanges conducted after solicitation issuance.

> **Manager Alert**
>
> Although contractors are part of the FAR-prescribed acquisition team, government planners must avoid both improprieties and the appearance of improprieties. While walking arm in arm with their acquisition partners (contractors), government personnel are still expected to keep the traditional arm's-length relationship.

Coordination of Activities

The FAR gives a great deal of latitude to program officials in conducting presolicitation exchanges with contractors, but the prudent program official may wish to keep agency contracting officials aware of any such presolicitation activities. This will help avoid any inadvertent violation of agency rules or policies.

Chapter 9

ESTABLISHING PROPOSAL EVALUATION FACTORS

Price or cost must, by law, be a consideration in all government source selections. But in addition to price or cost, procurement laws and regulations have long permitted consideration of non-cost factors. As previously stated, these factors are most commonly referred to as *merit factors* or *technical factors*. These non-cost evaluation factors may be used in both lowest price, technically acceptable (LPTA) and trade-off procurements.

FAR REQUIREMENTS

While both the regulations and legal precedent give government officials great latitude in choosing evaluation factors, FAR 15.304 does require that the following be addressed:

- **Quality.** Quality may be addressed through such factors as past performance, technical excellence, personnel, management capability, and experience.
- **Past performance.** The FAR provides that this requirement may be waived if the contracting officer documents why an evaluation of past performance would not be appropriate.
- **Use of various categories of small businesses.** If the proposed solicitation is to be unrestricted (that is, not set aside for a particular group of contractors such as small businesses or small disadvantaged businesses), then the proposed use of various categories of small businesses as subcontractors and vendors must be evaluated. This requirement applies to proposed contracts exceeding $650,000, unless they are construction

contracts, for which the threshold is $1.5 million. For Department of Defense (DoD) acquisitions, the plan may also address the use of historically black colleges and universities and other minority institutions as sources.

- **Use of small disadvantaged businesses.** For trade-off acquisitions exceeding the dollar thresholds noted above *and* within certain industry segments (identified by the Department of Commerce on an annual basis), agencies may include an evaluation factor regarding the use of small disadvantaged businesses.
- **Past performance in meeting small business subcontracting goals.** If the contract involves bundling (combining requirements that had previously been procured separately) and there is opportunity for subcontracting, the contracting officer must include a factor for evaluating competing contractor past performance in meeting small business subcontracting goals under previous contracts.

Additionally, for service contracts costing $650,000 or more that are expected to involve meaningful numbers of professional employees, FAR 22.1103 requires that compensation plans should be reviewed to determine whether they are unrealistically low.

EVALUATION FACTORS AND SUBFACTORS

Subfactors may be added under any non-cost evaluation factors. When using trade-off, the relative importance of both factors and significant subfactors must be determined and described in the solicitation.

Chosen factors and subfactors must

- Be tailored for the particular acquisition
- Represent the key areas of importance and emphasis upon which the source selection decision will be based
- Be definable, measurable, and stated in clearly understandable terms
- Support meaningful comparison and discrimination between competing contractors.

Selecting Non-Cost Factors

Two key areas are to be considered when acquisition planners establish non-cost factors. Foremost is the government requirements document, such as a statement of work, a performance work statement, or a statement of objectives. Second, and also of great import, is the information that has been obtained from market research and any presolicitation exchanges of information with contractors. This would include lessons learned from previous and similar efforts, names of contractors that are likely to compete, and knowledge about the state of the art in the relevant public sector.

The first question to be addressed by planners is "What should proposals contain to best ensure that a resultant contract would fully meet the government's needs?" For example, if the government is using a performance work statement or statement of objectives, would it be desirable to have competing contractors submit technical proposals in which they would explain in detail how they plan to do the work? If so, what exactly does the government need to properly judge the offerors' approach?

The result of contemplating these questions might be an evaluation factor that, in abbreviated form, looks something like this:

> **Technical Proposal.** The offeror shall submit a technical proposal addressing in a work breakdown structure (pursuant to Mil Std ___) how the offeror intends to meet the requirements of the performance work statement in Section C of the solicitation. Each paragraph of the performance work statement must be addressed. Proposals will be evaluated on the bases of completeness, feasibility, and risk. Risk assessment will include cost, schedule, and performance risk.

Presuming that the requirement is expected to result in a cost-reimbursement contract of significant monetary value, the planners may decide that they need to look at how the contractor is going to control costs while remaining on schedule. If so, they might include a factor that in an abbreviated form looks something like this:

> **Management Plan.** The offeror must furnish a management plan that encompasses earned value management techniques and demonstrates how cost and schedule will be monitored and controlled. The management plan must also include the processes that will be put into place to surface and resolve actual or projected deviations from projected costs and schedules. This includes identifying in the proposal the managerial level that will be involved in monitoring progress, participating in problem resolution, and overseeing any corrective actions necessary.
>
> As a separate part of the management plan, the offeror must indicate the proposed compensation plan for the professional employees expected to perform under any resultant contract.
>
> The management plan will be evaluated on the bases of feasibility, likelihood of success, and usefulness as a tool in risk management. The compensation portion will be reviewed to determine if compensation is of a level deemed reasonable for attracting and retaining highly qualified professionals.

The planners may also consider the qualifications of the key personnel to be used on the contract to be of great importance. If so, a "key personnel" evaluation factor could be used. For example, the government could explain the qualifications it is looking for and require offerors to provide a resume in a specified format for each of the key personnel who would perform the work under any resultant contract. Sometimes, to avoid a bait-and-switch situation, the government requires competing contractors to submit letters of intent to work from proposed key personnel.

Impact of Evaluation Factor Selection

Similar evaluation factors could be developed for past performance, experience, facilities and equipment, small business subcontracting, or any of a host of other potential evaluation factors. It is important to keep in mind, however, that:

- Each evaluation factor will require contractors to spend time and money preparing proposals and the government to spend time and money evaluating proposals.
- The FAR calls for factors that support meaningful comparison of, and discrimination between, competing contractors.
- The greater the number of evaluation factors used, the more likely it is that meaningful differences between contractors will not be readily apparent.

While it is important that the government include those factors essential to obtaining the best value under the trade-off process, or acceptable proposals under the LPTA process, it is clearly foolhardy to ask for too much. If market research indicates that only three potential contractors are expected to submit proposals and that all of them have more than adequate facilities and equipment, including "facilities and equipment" as an evaluation factor would probably not be a wise choice.

SAMPLE-ITIS

It is clear that some organizations suffer from "sample-itis." All of their new solicitations look surprisingly like all of their past solicitations, even when they address different requirements and different markets and were issued at different times. Succumbing to sample-itis—that is, copying from an old solicitation rather than tailoring evaluation factors to the current requirement and the results of market research—violates the FAR requirement that evaluation factors be tailored for each particular acquisition.

GREAT LATITUDE

Comptroller general protest decisions have given great latitude to agencies in determining what evaluation factors to use. Generally, the comptroller general will take the position that the agency is in the best position to determine what it needs, and the burden is on the protestor to conclusively demonstrate that an evaluation factor is unreasonable. The comptroller general has even found in favor of the government when an evaluation factor clearly gave the incumbent a substantial competitive edge. In Harbor Branch Oceanographic Institution, B-243417, July 17, 1991, the comptroller general opined, "As a general matter a competitive advantage gained through incumbency is not an unfair advantage that must be eliminated . . . rather, such an advantage is improper only where it results from preferential treatment of an offeror or other unfair action by the government."

The choices for selection of non-cost factors are virtually endless. Different groups of planners could look at the market research and the requirements document and develop completely different sets of evaluation factors. For example, instead of requiring a technical proposal, as was done in our hypothetical requirement discussed above, a group of planners might emphasize experience and past performance as non-cost evaluation factors and leave the question of how the job will be done to the competent contractor they will choose.

> **Manager Alert**
>
> Although we say this with some reluctance, there appears to be little doubt that evaluation factors can be skewed to favor or work against a particular contractor—an incumbent contractor, for example. Contracting officers, legal counsel, and the source selection authority are the primary lines of defense in making sure that factors chosen do not unduly favor one or more contractors. This does not mean that the project office is not permitted to ask for what it needs even if that has the impact of limiting competition. The Competition in Contracting Act allows restrictive requirements, but only to the "extent necessary." And in the 1991 comptroller general opinion cited above, the comptroller general wrote, "Where a solicitation includes requirements that restrict the ability of offerors to compete, the agency must have a reasonable basis for imposing the restrictive requirements." Thus an agency does not have to sacrifice needs in order to level the playing field for potential offerors. However, it must be prepared to conclusively demonstrate that the needs are genuine and reasonable.

WHERE TO BEGIN

There are a variety of ways to develop non-cost factors. For example, each individual acquisition planner (or member of the integrated product team) can independently review the government requirement and the information obtained from any market research, as well as any lessons learned from previous similar acquisitions. Then the team can meet and brainstorm what should or should not be included as an evaluation factor and whether any factors proposed should instead be subfactors. A consensus opinion reached can then be submitted for approval to the contracting officer and/or other source selection authority.

Another way to approach the matter is to have the senior planner from the project office propose evaluation factors and subfactors and then obtain team input and recommendations prior to seeking approval.

Whatever method an agency employs, it might be beneficial to keep in mind advice from the Department of Energy's Acquisition Guide (August 2004): "As a rule of thumb, evaluation criteria should reflect areas necessary to determine the merit of a proposal, pertinent to the Government's stated requirements and measurable to permit qualitative and quantitative assessment against the rating plan."

Chapter 10

SMALL BUSINESS PARTICIPATION AS A MERIT FACTOR

FAR Subpart 19.7 provides that solicitations for negotiated procurements in excess of $650,000 ($1.5 million for construction) must require contractors to commit to an acceptable small business subcontracting plan in order to receive a contract award. This requirement applies whenever there are "subcontracting opportunities." If the solicitation is set aside for competition only among small businesses, then a subcontracting plan is usually not required.

When a subcontracting plan is to be submitted by competing contractors, acquisition planners have to address exactly how this is to be accomplished. The law requires only that the contractor and the contracting officer agree to a satisfactory plan before a contract is awarded.

APPLICABLE FAR CLAUSE ALTERNATIVES

The standard FAR provision at 52.219-9, Small Business Subcontracting Plan (2011), allows the contracting officer to choose between different subparagraphs when placing the provision in a solicitation. One of the subparagraphs requires a competing contractor to submit a plan "upon the request of the contracting officer." Another requires that all competing large businesses submit such a plan as a part of their proposal.

In the first instance, the contracting officer could elect to ask only the apparent successful offeror for a plan. If the government and the contractor do not negotiate a satisfactory plan, then the contractor would not be eligible for award.

If the competing contractors are to be required to submit a subcontracting plan as part of their proposal, then acquisition planners, together with the contracting officer and agency small business advisors, must decide whether:
- The plans will be deemed "acceptable" or "not acceptable." This choice is available for both lowest price, technically acceptable and trade-off source selections.
- The plans will be scored or rated, a choice available only for trade-off source selections.

Additionally, source selection officials can either:
- Put target goals in the solicitation that competing contractors must meet, or
- Allow competing contractors to set their own proposed goals.

APPROVED SUBCONTRACTING PLANS

If a competing contractor already has an approved plan that covers its government business (a company or division plan called a *master plan* or *commercial plan*), that plan may be submitted as a part of the proposal or it may be referenced in the proposal.

AGENCY GUIDANCE

Although the above choices for evaluating subcontracting plans and the inclusion/exclusion of target goals are those available under law and general practice, each agency has internal guidance on these issues that is either mandatory or advisory. Government personnel must therefore review agency guidance before deciding among the choices available. Also, many agencies have prescribed forms or formats that competing contractors must use when submitting a small business subcontracting plan. When appropriate, this information must be included in the proposal submission instructions given to offerors in the solicitation.

SMALL DISADVANTAGED BUSINESS PARTICIPATION PROGRAM

FAR Subpart 19.12 also requires that a Small Disadvantaged Business (SDB) Participation Program provision be placed in solicitations for specific areas of industry identified annually by the Department of Commerce. The FAR requires that:

The solicitation shall describe the SDB participation evaluation factor or subfactor. The solicitation shall require offerors to provide, with their offers, targets, expressed as dollars and percentages of total contract value, in each of the applicable, authorized NAICS Industry Subsector[s], and a total target for SDB participation by the contractor, including joint venture partners, and team members, and a total target for SDB participation by subcontractors.

OTHER SOCIOECONOMIC EVALUATION FACTORS

Some agencies, such as some DoD components, may also include in solicitations a small business participation program requirement. All categories of businesses are asked to identify their subcontracting plans for various categories of small businesses and, where appropriate, historically black colleges and minority institutions.

> **Manager Alert**
> How and when these socioeconomically oriented evaluation factors are used can vary widely among agencies. Market research can play a large part in determining whether a requirement can be met if the competition is restricted to particular types of small businesses.

Chapter 11

ESTABLISHING PROPOSAL EVALUATION SUBFACTORS

FAR Part 15 requires that proposals be evaluated solely on the basis of the evaluation factors and significant subfactors that have been tailored for the specific acquisition and identified in the solicitation. It neither defines subfactors nor requires their use.

Government acquisition personnel normally use subfactors when they want to break out an evaluation factor into separate components to help offerors to better understand the factor, to make sure that important components of the evaluation factor are addressed in proposal preparation and proposal evaluation, and/or to establish the relative importance of the various components of the evaluation factor.

As an example, we can break out some of the components of the Management Plan factor mentioned in Chapter 9 into four subfactors. In an abbreviated fashion, such a breakdown might look something like this:

Management Plan
- Earned value management
- Key personnel
- Employee compensation plan
- Involvement of contractor management

Note that in the above example, *Key personnel*, which previously was discussed as a potential stand-alone evaluation factor, has been made a subfactor under Management Plan. This further demonstrates the broad flexibility that acquisition planners have in establishing factors and subfactors. Any number of factors and subfactors can be used, with almost limitless choices available to those developing the evaluation factors.

When using the trade-off process, the government must convey to offerors the relative importance of factors and subfactors. In turn, offerors must address each factor and subfactor in their proposals, and government evaluators must consider them and their relative importance when evaluating the proposals.

> **Manager Alert**
>
> There is no governmentwide template for determining and developing factors and subfactors. It is purely a judgment call for agency acquisition officials. Two different groups of planners could look at an identical situation and come to widely different conclusions about the factors and subfactors (if any) that should be used.
>
> If a contractor protests the factors or subfactors used in a solicitation, the government must demonstrate a reasonable basis for the choices made. If a reasonable basis is shown, the comptroller general and the courts usually will not substitute their judgment for the judgment of agency officials.

Chapter 12

ESTABLISHING THE RELATIVE IMPORTANCE OF EVALUATION FACTORS AND SUBFACTORS

FAR 15.304 requires that the evaluation factors and subfactors that will affect contract award, as well as their relative importance, be clearly stated in the solicitation. There are sound reasons for this requirement. It helps the government get the types of proposals it seeks, and it aids contractors in preparing their proposals by identifying the areas they should emphasize. Further, it can influence the contractor decision whether to submit a proposal at all. If, for example, past performance is significantly more important than all other non-cost factors, a contractor with a marginal past performance record may decide that it would be a waste of time and money to prepare a proposal, as the chances of receiving an award would be minimal.

LOWEST PRICE, TECHNICALLY ACCEPTABLE EXCLUDED

When lowest price, technically acceptable (LPTA) is to be used, there is no need to identify the relative importance of evaluation factors and subfactors. If a responsible contractor is acceptable on all factors, it will receive the award if it has the lowest price or cost.

DISCRETION OF PLANNERS

Just as they do when establishing evaluation factors, acquisition officials have broad discretion in determining their relative importance. Again, two separate groups of acquisition officials could come to two different conclusions.

DESCRIBING RELATIVE IMPORTANCE

How relative importance will be reflected in the solicitation is also a matter of choice. In the past, it was common practice to use numerical scoring. Although there was no requirement that they do so, the numbers assigned (i.e., maximum scores) for individual evaluation factors almost always added up to 100 or some multiple of 100 (such as 500 or 1,000). The following is an example:

Factor 1: Technical Approach	**50 points**
Feasibility	25 points
Completeness	25 points
Factor 2: Key Personnel	**25 points**
Factor 3: Management Plan	**25 points**
Cost control	15 points
Schedule control	10 points

Over the years, describing relative importance by using numbers fell out of favor with most agencies. It implied a degree of precision that is not inherent in the relatively subjective source trade-off process.

Today it is far more common to use broader characterizations of relative importance. For example, instead of using numbers to describe relative importance as shown above, a solicitation might say something like this:

> Technical Approach is most important and is significantly more important than Key Personnel. Key Personnel is equal in importance to Management Plan. Subfactors A and B under Technical Approach are equal in importance. Of the subfactors under Management Plan, Subfactor A is more important than Subfactor B.

This meets the FAR requirement for disclosing relative importance. However, this approach does have a downside insofar as contractors are concerned. Imagine if there were ten or 20 evaluation factors instead of only three, and if there were dozens of subfactors. Explaining the relative importance of each of these factors and subfactors as we have done here can result in a solicitation (i.e., RFP) provision that is convoluted and difficult to understand. It is not without justification that some contractors call this part of the solicitation "the riddle." If the planning team is going to pose a riddle, it is to everyone's advantage to make it a riddle that is easy to solve.

> **Manager Alert**
>
> Some agencies routinely describe the relative importance of factors and subfactors by simply saying that they are listed in descending order of importance. This can be an effective explanation when there are more or less uniform gradients between the factors and subfactors— or, to put it another way, when they reflect a reasonable downward progression. However, this phrasing should not be used without further clarification for situations like the one described above. Note that in the above example, there are no uniform gradients between factors, nor is there a reasonable downward progression of the factors. In fact, one factor is significantly more important than either of the others, which are equal in importance.
>
> If an agency wishes to "protest-proof" a source selection process, it should be careful to use the phrase "descending order of importance" without any further clarification only when it is reasonably descriptive of the actual order of importance.

WHEN RELATIVE IMPORTANCE IS NOT SPECIFIED

On a number of occasions, the comptroller general has opined in protest decisions that competing contractors have a right to assume that evaluation factors or subfactors are equal in importance when the government fails to identify their relative importance in the solicitation.

THE IMPACT OF RELATIVE IMPORTANCE

Once relative importance is established in the solicitation, the government must make decisions consistent with the promises made. It should not, for example, indicate that past performance will be the most significant factor in a source selection and then make a selection decision in which past performance evaluation played little or no role.

WHAT IF?

When establishing evaluation factors and their relative importance, it may be helpful to go through some mental gymnastics known as *what if*. For example, if the government intends to make technical approach far more important than key personnel and past performance, government planners could ask themselves, "What if we get an attractively priced proposal with some really great technical ideas from a contractor with undistinguished key personnel and a so-so past performance rating? Is that what we really want?"

Chapter 13

SELECTING A RATING METHOD

Typically, when proposals are evaluated for trade-off they receive a score or rating of some sort, to aid the contracting officer and/or source selection authority (SSA) in determining the competitive range (if discussions are to be held) and in selecting the successful contractor(s). It's important to note, however, that the scores themselves do not bind the contracting officer or other SSA; they are simply considered to be guides for them and for other source selection officials.

The FAR does not refer to "scoring" per se, but instead calls the scoring process a "rating method." FAR 15.305(a) permits any rating method or combination of methods, including:

- Numerical weights
- Color ratings
- Adjectival ratings
- Ordinal ratings.

USING NUMBERS

At one time, it was common to assign proposals numerical ratings or scores, but this sometimes made it difficult to make a true best value decision when using the trade-off process. This was especially true when proposed cost received a score. To illustrate this point, consider the hypothetical factor and subfactor weighting shown in the last chapter.

Factor 1: Technical Approach	**50 points**
Feasibility	25 points
Completeness	25 points

Factor 2: Key Personnel	25 points
Factor 3: Management Plan	25 points
Cost control	15 points
Schedule control	10 points

Now let us also assume that we have decided to give cost or price a maximum of 50 points (one of several methods that have been used for scoring cost). When we are at the point of making the award decision, we find that the three remaining competitors have scores and costs as follows:

Contractor	Score for Non-Cost Factors	Cost
Contractor A	90 points	$1,875,000
Contractor B	87 points	$1,687,500
Contractor C	80 points	$1,500,000

Because proposal A's cost is 25 percent higher than the lowest cost, its cost score is reduced by 25 percent. It receives 37.5 points of the maximum 50. Since B's cost is 12.5 percent higher than the lowest cost, its cost score is reduced by 12.5 percent, and it receives 43.75 points. C offers the lowest cost and so receives all 50 points. Thus the final scores are as follows:

Contractor	Final Scores
Contractor A	90 + 37.5 = 127.50
Contractor B	87 + 43.75 = 130.75
Contractor C	80 + 50.00 = 130.00

No business judgment is applied and the contractor with the highest total score receives the award. Obviously, this method led to some poor source selection decisions, and thus the practice of scoring costs fell into disfavor.

The above method was not the only way that costs were scored. Some agencies used sophisticated algebraic equations to perform a "best buy analysis" wherein the winner was chosen by a price analyst or some other knowledgeable person who could understand the equation.

Even though most agencies drifted away from the practice of scoring costs, the practice of using numbers to rate non-cost factors continued in many agencies. This too led to some untenable situations. Consider a situation in which two competing contractors have final scores and proposed costs as follows:

Contractor	Score for Non-Cost Factors	Cost
Contractor A	90 points	$900,000
Contractor B	86 points	$1,000,000

The SSA and his or her advisors have noted that contractor B is planning to use the top scientist in the country as the principal investigator, so they would really prefer to give the award to B. However, awarding to the lowest-rated contractor at the highest cost might be a very difficult (but not impossible) decision to defend. Perhaps if they had weighted key personnel more heavily, the scores would have come out differently. But they did not, so they have to live with the consequences.

USING ADJECTIVES OR COLORS

In part to avoid similar difficult situations, agencies began to embrace rating methods that characterized proposals in a less-specific fashion than using numbers. For example, proposals could receive a rating of "outstanding," "highly acceptable," "acceptable," or "not acceptable" instead of receiving a numerical rating or score.

In the above example, both contractors would probably be rated "highly acceptable," and the SSA could readily pick contractor B merely by explaining in the source selection decision that the exceptional expertise to be gained was worth the additional cost.

Some agencies use color ratings instead of adjectives, but the impact is essentially the same. They reflect broad ranges of suitability rather than a precise number. Below is a simplified example of a color rating scheme:

Color	Rating
Blue	Surpasses government minimum requirements
Green	Meets government requirements
Yellow	Not acceptable, but susceptible to being made acceptable through discussions
Red	Not acceptable; not reasonably susceptible to being made acceptable through discussions

VARIATIONS ON COMMON RATING METHODS

In addition to the rating methods identified in the FAR, agencies have used symbols (such as plus signs and minus signs), narrative descriptions, and various combinations of the approaches we have discussed. Some apply both qualitative ratings (e.g., "outstanding," "marginal") and risk ratings (e.g., "high risk," "low risk") to the evaluation factors.

Some have used numbers to score technical proposals and have adjusted these numbers using the notion of expected value based on an adjudged confidence level after evaluation of past performance. For example, presume contractor A received 90 technical points and has a superb past performance rating (confidence assessment score) of 100 percent. Contractor B received 95 technical points but has a past performance-based confidence score of only 80 percent. Their scores would be as follows:

Contractor	Proposal Score		Confidence Assessment Score	Rating
Contractor A	90	×	100%	90
Contractor B	95	×	80%	76

Unless restricted by agency regulations, agency officials have broad discretion in developing rating schemes. They can design a scheme that encourages proposals from the types of contractors they would prefer to have compete and discourages proposals from less qualified contractors by, for example, emphasizing past performance or experience, or by setting specific minimum requirements, such as requiring that researchers have a doctorate in a particular discipline.

> **Manager Alert**
> Regardless of the method of scoring or rating chosen, it is important that the meanings of the various adjectives, colors, or other chosen rating methods be carefully and uniformly defined for evaluators to improve consistency among evaluators in how the rating method is applied.

Chapter 14

PAST PERFORMANCE AS AN EVALUATION FACTOR

For many years contracting officers used past performance only to determine whether a contractor had the ability and the demonstrated will to do the job—that is, to determine whether the contractor was a responsible contractor and thus eligible for award.

A contractor with outstanding past performance had no competitive advantage over a contractor with adequate past performance.

PAST PERFORMANCE VS. EXPERIENCE

Past performance as a non-cost evaluation factor differs somewhat from experience. Basically, experience addresses *what* work the contractor has done, while past performance addresses *how well* the contractor performed. However, the government normally looks not just at past performance but also at the relevancy of that past performance—in other words, the type of experience—when making source selection decisions.

A HARD NUT TO CRACK

In various attempts to make government source selection more efficient, one aspect of the government acquisition process was a particularly hard nut to crack. Most private-sector buyers carefully choose the sources from which they will solicit proposals and often try to establish long-term business relationships with dependable suppliers. With limited exceptions, the government is required by the Competition in Contracting Act to solicit offers from every Tom, Dick, and Harriet who wishes to compete for a government requirement. Further, with respect to long-term relationships, the government may not "favor" one contractor over another. These governmental constraints add time and expense to the source selection process.

In an effort to improve these aspects of the source selection process, the government began to use past performance as a significant non-cost evaluation factor. Through emphasis on past performance, the government could discourage poor or marginal contractors from submitting proposals, since they would have little or no chance of receiving award. And the use of past performance could encourage those who already have contracts to do well in order to improve the opportunity for future contracts.

The Office of Federal Procurement Policy opined in its *Best Practices for Collecting and Using Current and Past Performance Information* (May 2000) that no other non-cost factor should be considered more important than past performance. There is merit in this opinion. If there is such a thing as a successful horse-racing bettor, it is likely to be one who looks closely at past performance before investing money. Long shots may rise to the occasion, but you can't depend on them.

ADDRESSING CONCERNS ABOUT THE USE OF PAST PERFORMANCE

Seldom has any change in the source selection process caused as much widespread concern among contractors and acquisition officials as did the emphasis on past performance. Most of these concerns were alleviated by the government through:

- Providing a mechanism wherein contractors could appeal government past performance reports at a level higher than the contracting officer. This addressed contractors' concerns that a single unfair performance report could severely impact their continuing competitive status.
- Considering the currency and relevancy of past performance information obtained when evaluating contractors. This addressed contractor concerns that past performance from many years ago would come back to haunt them even though they had taken corrective action and improved their performance.
- Developing a governmentwide database (the Past Performance Information Retrieval System). This addressed some government acquisition officials' concerns about the difficulty of obtaining reliable, consistent, and relevant past performance data.
- Addressing in the FAR and in case law how competing contractors with no relevant past performance will be rated. Some likened this situation to the difficulty that young job seekers face when they cannot get a job without experience but cannot get experience without a job.

- Providing in the FAR that past performance need not be evaluated if the contracting officer documents the reason past performance is not an appropriate factor for the acquisition. This addressed government acquisition officials' concerns about being compelled to use an evaluation factor that might not be appropriate for a specific acquisition.

> **Manager Alert**
>
> There is one very substantive difference in how past performance is used as an evaluation factor in lowest price, technically acceptable (LPTA) as opposed to how it is used in trade-off. In LPTA, contractors are rated either "acceptable" or "unacceptable" on the evaluation factors. Thus, a contractor that is deemed "not acceptable" under an LPTA past performance factor is, in effect, being found to be "not responsible" and is therefore not eligible to receive a contract award.
>
> When a small business is found to be "not responsible" by the contracting officer, it may appeal to the Small Business Administration (SBA) for a certificate of competency (COC), pursuant to FAR Subpart 19.6, and still have an opportunity to receive a contract award. Businesses do not have this particular right of appeal in a trade-off selection just because they were rated lower than other contractors on a past performance evaluation factor. In that case, the government is not making a determination of responsibility; it is merely categorizing the relative quality of the past performance of competing contractors.

PLANNING CONCERNS

Among the matters related to evaluating past performance that the planning team will have to address, subject to the approval of the contracting officer and/or other source selection authority, are the following:

- Whether to include past performance as an evaluation factor
- The relative weight to be given to past performance (if it is a trade-off solicitation)
- The rating/scoring method to be used
- Whether a separate group, such as a performance risk assessment group, will evaluate past performance
- The instructions that will be given in the solicitation to guide offerors in submitting past performance information

- Instructions given to evaluators and the forms (such as past performance questionnaires) evaluators will use.

FAR GUIDANCE

Unlike the limited guidance it provides regarding any other non-cost factors, the FAR has relatively detailed guidance on the use of past performance information as an evaluation factor. This guidance, found in 15.305, states that:

- The solicitation shall describe the approach for evaluating past performance.
- The solicitation shall also authorize offerors to provide information on problems encountered on relevant past contracts.
- The evaluation of past performance should include the past performance of offerors with respect to subcontracting plan goals for small disadvantaged business (SDB) concerns.

Chapter 15

THE RELATIVE IMPORTANCE OF COST

As previously stated, cost must be a factor in all source selections. The relative importance of cost in a selection may vary depending upon the unique characteristics of the requirement. For example, we might feel comfortable buying standard commercial items on the basis of the lowest price available, but not so comfortable if we were stuck with the low bid in procuring the services of a heart surgeon.

FAR REQUIREMENTS

For trade-off source selections, FAR 15.304 requires that the solicitation (the request for proposals or other solicitation document) state, as a minimum, whether all evaluation factors other than cost or price when combined are:

- Significantly more important than cost or price
- Approximately equal to cost or price
- Significantly less important than cost or price.

Accordingly, acquisition planners have to decide the relative importance of cost or price. For most trade-off procurements, agencies tend to opt for "significantly more important than cost or price." This gives a great deal of flexibility to the source selection authority (SSA) because, notwithstanding the emphasis on cost or price, the SSA can choose a lower-priced proposal if he or she does not think that an increase in proposal merit is worth the corresponding increase in price.

Some agencies have a practice of informing offerors that "as merit tends to equalize, cost may become a more significant factor," as it is often phrased. Although arguably unnecessary, these kinds of commonsense qualifying statements probably do no harm and may help competing contractors better understand the process.

THE CONTINUUM OF IMPORTANCE

FAR 15.101 describes a continuum on which the relative importance of cost or price may vary. It states, as an example, that "in acquisitions where the requirement is clearly definable and the risk of successful contractor performance is minimal, cost or price may play a dominant role in source selection. The less definitive the requirement, the more development work required, or the greater the performance risk, the more technical or past performance may play a dominant role." The FAR offers this information only as an "example," so presumably the desire or need for *quality* could also be a factor in determining the relative importance of price or cost.

> **Manager Alert**
> Cost (or price) must *always* be a factor in source selection, but it need not be the most significant factor. Agencies must be sensitive, however, to an apparent growing public perception that the government sometimes spends a significant amount of monies for only marginal increases in quality.

Chapter 16

DESIGNING PROPOSAL PREPARATION INSTRUCTIONS

Each solicitation must include instructions to offerors that identify the format to be used by competing contractors in preparing proposals and must identify the matters to be addressed in the proposal. These instructions almost always specify the order in which offerors are to present the information.

There are virtually no regulatory constraints placed on planners in developing proposal preparation instructions. Government planners should make good business decisions and develop instructions that fully meet government needs without unduly adding to contractor cost in preparing proposals.

STANDARD PRACTICE

Typically, competing contractors are asked to submit proposals in at least two parts:
1. The technical/merit proposal
2. The cost proposal.

This request is made because one assigned group or person usually evaluates the technical (or merit) proposal and another assigned group or individual evaluates the cost or price proposal. This two-part submission also accommodates the common practice of keeping cost information away from technical/merit evaluators until after their evaluation is complete. Ostensibly this is done so that these evaluators will consider only the technical/merit factors and will not be unduly influenced by cost or price. Although it is common practice to have the cost proposal submitted separately, the FAR does not require that this be done.

VARIATIONS

When different groups or individuals are to be assigned to evaluate discrete aspects of the non-cost factors, competing contractors may be required to submit proposals in more than two separate parts, often called *volumes*. For example, in an Air Force acquisition involving the environmental remediation of 14 Air Force bases, competing contractors were permitted to submit offers to remediate just one site, all sites, or any number in between. They were asked to submit proposals in separate volumes to facilitate evaluation by separate groups. These volumes were:

Volume I	Executive summary
Volume II	Technical proposal
Volume III	Management proposal
Volume IV	Site-specific information
Volume V	Past performance
Volume VI	Administrative proposal
Volume VII	Cost proposal

Of course, the Air Force provided specific instructions about what was to be included in each volume.

MEDIA TO BE USED

The government can require that proposals, or parts of proposals, be submitted on paper, on disk or video/audio tape, and/or as an oral presentation. Agencies may specify requirements for font size, paper size, margins, or length, and they may also impose other restrictions or offer additional guidance.

ISSUES TO CONSIDER

There are a number of issues government planners must consider when designing proposal preparation instructions. Foremost, the instructions have to be compatible with the requirements document and with the proposal evaluation factors. The government has to have the information it needs to evaluate proposals in the manner promised in the solicitation and to ultimately determine which proposal offers the best value. Secondly, the instructions should be designed to permit an efficient evaluation process. For example, it is useful to specify the order in which offerors are to present information so that there will be uniformity among proposals and evaluators will not have to search through the proposals for specific required information. Limits on size and content can also facilitate evaluation, since evaluators will not have to wade through trade puffery of questionable value in order to ferret out meaningful content.

Specific proposal preparation instructions can also level the playing field among contractors. If instructions limit the size and content of proposals, competing contractors will not have to guess what the government wants or strive to make a favorable impression by outspending one another in developing lengthy, elaborate proposals.

> **Manager Alert**
>
> There have been a number of successful contractor protests regarding the incompatibility of proposal preparation instructions with the requirements document (statement of work) and/or the evaluation factors. Providing instructions that are consistent with all parts of the solicitation is a job to be taken seriously. Be careful about the sample-itis that we warned against in Chapter 9.

USE OF MARKET RESEARCH

Market research should play a part in the design of the proposal preparation instructions, just as it does in establishing evaluation criteria. In one highly publicized acquisition, a government agency indicated in its proposal instructions that all offerors would be given an opportunity to give an oral presentation after written proposals were received and that the oral presentations would be evaluated. The agency apparently expected a modest number of written proposals when it designed these instructions, but it actually received more than 200 written proposals. Giving hundreds of offerors an opportunity to deliver an evaluated oral presentation would have consumed an onerous amount of time. Consequently, the agency did not give all offerors an opportunity to give an oral presentation, but instead devised a modified evaluation scheme wherein only selected offerors had that opportunity. The agency did this without amending the request for proposals (RFP) to revise the evaluation criteria and the proposal preparation instructions.

Not surprisingly, this provoked multiple protests. The comptroller general upheld the protests and recommended that the agency either afford all offerors an opportunity to give an oral presentation or amend the RFP and allow offerors to revise their proposals (Kathpal Technologies, Inc.; Computer & Hi-Tech Management, Inc., B-283137.3, December 30, 1999). The outcome for the agency was the loss of a considerable amount of time, energy, and money.

Perhaps more extensive market research that included contacting the private sector through requests for information or draft RFPs would have disclosed the high degree of interest in the acquisition and caused planners to design more appropriate proposal preparation instructions. Or perhaps some "what-if" gymnastics would have been in order during the planning phase. Planners could have asked themselves, "What if we receive a large number of proposals?"

Chapter 17

ORAL PRESENTATIONS

Oral presentations, which were sometimes called oral proposals, began to be used in earnest in the 1980s during a period of great change and experimentation in the source selection process. This experimentation was intended to both improve the effectiveness of source selections and streamline the source selection process. Most of the streamlining efforts were aimed at reducing the expense associated with the source selection process and the amount of time the process consumed.

Initially, procurement reformers in the government and the private sector believed that substituting oral presentations for written material offered a substantial opportunity for streamlining the process. However, during the experimentation phase, many contracting officers and other source selection officials found oral presentations to be most valuable when they augmented rather than substituted for written material. They felt that this approach gave them far greater insight into the written material and allowed for more accurate proposal evaluations and better source selection decisions. Ironically, however, the use of oral presentations in those cases actually added time and expense to the process. For example, instead of just submitting a written proposal, a contractor might also be required to prepare a slide show and fly to Paducah to present it to the government. Government evaluators also were affected, since they had to spend more time on the evaluation process.

In a relatively rare occurrence of regulation following practice, oral presentations were widely used throughout federal executive agencies before they were covered in the FAR. Ultimately, oral presentation guidance was added to FAR Part 15. That guidance allowed for oral presentations to be used either to substitute for or to augment written material.

AN OPPORTUNITY FOR DIALOGUE

Because the FAR makes it clear that oral presentations provide an opportunity for *dialogue* between the government and competing contractors, prerecorded presentations are not considered oral presentations. There is no prohibition against conveying proposal information to the government in this manner if it is allowed by or required by the solicitation, but these formats are not considered oral presentations.

"JOB INTERVIEW"

It is normal practice for government agencies to require that oral presentations be given by one or more of the key people who are slated to work on the contract, such as the offeror's proposed project officer or senior scientist. Thus, some government program officials refer to oral presentations as "job interviews" because the officials will have the opportunity to judge the competence and demeanor of the persons with whom they may be working in the months ahead.

POP QUIZZES

Some agencies use a "pop quiz" technique during oral presentations wherein presenters are asked questions about the general subject area of the contract. For example, if the contract requirement is for environmental remediation, the presenter(s) may be asked questions about hazardous waste disposal or some other important aspect of environmental remediation. The point of quizzing the presenters is, of course, to ascertain if they know what they are talking about. And perhaps to judge their professional demeanor.

If presenters are to be evaluated on the basis of a pop quiz, the solicitation must indicate that this is planned.

When the government was just beginning to use oral presentations in source selection, some championed them as a sorely needed device for making better source selections. They argued that the reliance on written proposals was turning source selection into an essay-writing contest. But others were concerned that the charisma and presentation skills of presenters could just as easily unduly influence evaluators. The pop quiz technique is seen as one way to guard against that happening.

TIME FOR PRESENTATIONS

Time is an important issue when planning for oral presentations. Some oral presentations have lasted just 30 minutes, while others have lasted a day and a half or more. The ability of evaluators to maintain an effective level of concentration over time should be considered by government planners when establishing presentation time requirements. In many cases, shorter may be better.

Other issues to be considered in planning for oral presentations include:

- **Location.** If presentations are to be given at a government location, planners should select a location that is readily accessible to contractors, that will be available when needed, and where disruptions are unlikely to occur.
- **Equipment.** If presentations are to be given at a government location, the solicitation should identify the equipment available for contractor use when giving the presentation. Furthermore, someone in the government should make sure the necessary equipment is available at the promised time and is suitable for use. It may also be wise to have standby equipment available.
- **Number of attendees.** The solicitation should address the number of contractor attendees that will be permitted to attend the oral presentation in addition to the required or permitted presenters.
- **Order of presentation.** Most competing contractors want to present their material either first or last, since behavioral research indicates that material presented first or last in a lineup makes a stronger impression than material presented in the middle. To be fair to competing contractors, most agencies determine the order of presentation through a lottery procedure (such as drawing names out of a hat). Competing contractors are usually informed in the solicitation when this will be the case.
- **Recording of presentations.** The government is required to maintain a record of oral presentations. The method of establishing the record and the level of detail in the record are at the discretion of the source selection authority. However, it is suggested that the government not rely on briefing slides alone as the required record. Few things are more ambiguous than the bullets on a briefing slide when there is no one there to explain them.
- **Time of evaluation.** Planners will have to decide how and when evaluators will evaluate the presentations. Generally, evaluations will be more accurate if they are done immediately after each presentation. If evaluations are not to be done until all presentations have been given, then it is suggested that presentations be electronically recorded so that evaluators can refresh their memories before rating or scoring individual presentations.
- **Rescheduling.** Planners will have to decide whether to permit any rescheduling and, if it is to be allowed, the circumstances under which rescheduling will be considered.

Obviously, planners must address a significant number of issues when considering the use of oral presentations. This should not deter planners from using this valuable tool when it can contribute to an effective source selection.

DIALOGUE AND DISCUSSIONS

As shown in Exhibit 2-1 and Figures 2-1 and 2-2, the government may make an award based on either of the following:
- Initial proposals received without conducting discussions
- Final proposal revisions obtained after holding discussions.

The FAR anticipates that there will be dialogue between the government and competing contractors when the contractors give oral presentations (FAR 15.102). This "dialogue" will not be considered to be discussions unless it gives the contractor an opportunity to change its proposal. Thus, controlled dialogue could take place during oral presentations and award could still be made on the basis of initial proposals, including any oral presentations, without the government's holding actual discussions and receiving revised proposals.

> **Manager Alert**
> If discussions are held with one contractor in the competitive range, they must be held with all contractors in the competitive range. Thus, if discussions take place at one oral presentation, discussions may also have to be held with other competitive contractors.

Chapter 18

ADVERTISING A PLANNED ACQUISITION

Public law requires that proposed contract actions expected to exceed $25,000 be publicized on a government website called Federal Business Opportunities, or FedBizOpps (www.fedbizopps.gov), the governmentwide point of entry. Agencies publicize these contract actions by furnishing a synopsis (a brief description of the proposed action) that can readily be accessed by contractors. FAR 5.207 provides very specific content requirements for synopses. See Exhibit 18-1 for an example of a rather straightforward synopsis. The example shown makes clear to potential contractors the purpose of the contract, where contract performance will take place, and when contract performance will be required.

FAR 5.203(a) requires that a synopsis for most planned procurements be published at least 15 days before the solicitation is issued; a shorter lead time is permitted for commercial item acquisitions.

GOALS OF THE SYNOPSIS REQUIREMENT

The goals of the synopsis requirement are to increase competition, broaden industry participation in government requirements, and help certain socioeconomic categories of contractors in obtaining government contracts and subcontracts. These certain categories include small businesses, veteran-owned businesses, small disadvantaged businesses, women-owned businesses, and small businesses located in historically underutilized business areas (HUBZone businesses).

When a contractor reviews a synopsis and determines that it has a reasonable potential for submitting a winning proposal, it will request an opportunity to participate in the procurement. Accordingly, synopses should be carefully worded to attract offerors that could feasibly furnish the product or service and not unfairly encourage proposals from those who would have little or no chance of receiving a contract award.

EXCEPTIONS TO THE SYNOPSIS REQUIREMENT

There are 15 exceptions to the synopsis requirement:
1. National security issues.
2. Unusual urgency.
3. Certain procurements on behalf of foreign governments or pursuant to international agreements.
4. Procurements authorized or required by statute to be made through another government agency.
5. Utility services (other than telecommunications) where only one source is available.
6. Orders placed under indefinite delivery contracts.
7. Actions under the Small Business Innovation Development Act of 1982.
8. Procurements resulting from unsolicited proposals under which a synopsis would improperly disclose original, innovative, or proprietary information.
9. Certain actions for perishable subsistence supplies.
10. Certain brand-name items intended for resale.
11. Certain actions under contracts previously synopsized.
12. Defense agency contracts performed outside of the United States and its outlying areas and for which only local sources will be solicited.
13. Certain simplified acquisitions to which the public may respond electronically.
14. Certain expert services involving litigation or dispute.
15. An agency head has made a written determination that advance notice is not appropriate or reasonable. (This requires consultation with the administrator of the Office of Federal Procurement Policy and the administrator of the Small Business Administration).

OTHER SITUATIONS IN WHICH SYNOPSES ARE USED

In addition to advertising a planned procurement, in certain special situations advertising at FedBizOpps may be either permitted or required:

- Research and development "sources sought" notices, which are used when market research does not identify a sufficient number of potential contractors to obtain adequate competition
- Establishing or changing the mission of a federally funded research center

- Issuing notices of events related to procurement, such as business fairs, long-range procurement planning meetings, and preproposal conferences
- Certain architect-engineer service acquisitions
- Private-public competitions
- Small disadvantaged business competitive acquisitions under Section 8(a) of the Small Business Act
- Notices of draft requests for proposals or requests for information.

COMBINED SOLICITATION/SYNOPSIS

FAR Part 12 permits a combined synopsis/solicitation for commercial items. When this is done, there is no need to prepare or issue a separate solicitation. This procedure is further discussed in Chapter 35.

EXHIBIT 18-1
Sample Synopsis: Veterans Administration Health Services Procurement

Solicitation Number:
VA25710RP0201

Notice Type:
Solicitation

VA North Texas Health Care System has a requirement for Home Health Care Services. Contractor shall provide in-Home Health Care to Veteran beneficiaries located within the following Texas & Oklahoma counties:

Cooke, Delta, Fannin, Grayson, Hopkins, Hunt, Lamar, Red River counties

Bryan and Choctaw counties (Bryan and Choctaw are located in Oklahoma.)

Levels of care shall include Skilled Nursing, Homemaker Services, Home Health Aide, Physical Therapy, Speech Therapy and Occupational Therapy.

The contract shall be effective for a base period beginning on award date and continuing through 06/30/20__, with two one-year option periods available.

The NAICS code for this requirement is 621610 and the SBA size standard is $13,500,000.

Anticipated solicitation issued date will be on or about 06/02/20__ with the closing date of 06/23/20__, and will be issued as a commercial item requirement. Interested parties may obtain a copy of this solicitation number VA-257-10-RP-0201 at the following URL: http://www.fedbizopps.gov.

Source: www.fbo.gov/spg/VA/VANTHCS/VANTHCS/VA25710RP0201/listing.html.

Chapter 19

PREPARING THE SOLICITATION

When planning has been completed and the choices among the alternatives discussed in the previous chapters have been made, a solicitation is prepared. The uniform contract format (UCF), shown in Exhibit 19-1, is the format used for most conventional source selections using requests for proposals (RFPs). Although other formats are used for specific purposes, such as the solicitation/contract format for commercial items, all formats have these common elements relating to the source selection process:

- They define the requirement.
- They give proposal preparation instructions as appropriate.
- They inform potential offerors of the evaluation factors and any subfactors and, if it is a trade-off source selection, the relative importance of those factors and subfactors.

It is critical to the source selection process that these and other key elements of the solicitation be compatible. For example, you cannot evaluate a competing contractor's technical approach unless you first ask the contractor to furnish a technical approach as a part of its proposal. And you would not consider technical approach at all if the requirements document specified that the contractor must use a government-mandated technical approach.

> **Manager Alert**
>
> While it may seem to be common sense that solicitation content needs to be internally consistent, issues related to a lack of consistency have caused many significant problems in the past. This is why FAR 15.303 now specifically requires that the source selection authority *shall* "ensure consistency among the solicitation requirements, notices to offerors, proposal preparation instructions, evaluation factors and subfactors, solicitation provisions or contract clauses, and data requirements."

INSTRUCTIONS TO OFFERORS

A solicitation must also include a variety of clauses and provisions that are required by the FAR and agency regulations. This requirement is fulfilled by either including in the solicitation the clauses and provisions in toto or by referring to the particular FAR part or other government document where the clause or provision can be found.

One of these standard provisions, Instructions to Offerors—Competitive Acquisitions (FAR 52.215-1), is especially important in the source selection process. The current version of this provision appears in Exhibit 19-2. As may be seen in the exhibit, subparagraph (f)(4) of the standard provision informs competing contractors that the government intends to make an award without establishing a competitive range and without holding discussions. However, that subparagraph also gives the government the right to change its mind and hold discussions if the contracting officer later decides it is necessary.

An alternate subparagraph (f)(4) may be used if the government intends to establish a competitive range and hold discussions. The contracting officer and the source selection authority will determine which of these subparagraphs to use when the solicitation is prepared.

Other matters covered in the provision in Exhibit 19-2 include information/rules regarding late proposals, withdrawal of proposals, marking of proprietary/protected data, alternate proposals, and debriefing information.

COMPATIBILITY AND CLARITY

It is essential that the solicitation be carefully prepared and that all source selection provisions be clearly written. See Appendix I for an example of a Section L and a Section M that were used in a Department of Defense solicitation.

Because acquisition planners will have already done the lion's share of determining what goes in Sections L and M of the UCF when they reach the point of preparing the solicitation, the only major task remaining is to integrate the information into the solicitation in a way that ensures clarity and compatibility with other parts of the solicitation. This can be especially challenging if different authors have written different sections of the RFP, if individual section content has been designed by committee, or if the contracting organization "cuts and pastes" material from past solicitations into the new solicitation.

SPECIAL STANDARDS

The example solicitation excerpt in Appendix I contains a noteworthy requirement in that competing contractors must meet certain security standards in order to be considered responsible contractors. FAR 9.104-2 provides the following:

> When it is necessary for a particular acquisition or class of acquisitions, the contracting officer shall develop, with the assistance of appropriate specialists, special standards of responsibility. Special standards may be particularly desirable when experience has demonstrated that unusual expertise or specialized facilities are needed for adequate contract performance. The special standards shall be set forth in the solicitation (and so identified) and shall apply to all offerors.

When special standards are to be used, it is a good idea to put them in Section M. Potential contractors pay particular attention to the evaluation factors in Section M to help them determine whether to compete. Of course, they also look at Section C to see if they can do the work required at a profit and at Section L to judge the cost of competing.

CAREFUL PREPARATION AND PROOFREADING

Under normal circumstances, much of the content of a solicitation becomes the contract. In fact, when using the UCF, only sections L and M are used solely for source selection. It is critical that the entire solicitation be carefully prepared and that it be as unambiguous as the government can make it. The draft solicitation should be read multiple times by different people to identify and revise any ambiguous language. Remember that the parties have to live with the solicitation promises made to, and instructions given to, competing contractors during the source selection process. And the parties will be legally bound by the resultant contract.

MAKING THE SOLICITATION AVAILABLE

The solicitation is made available to contractors on any agency source list and to all contractors that have properly responded to the synopsis. In some cases, the agency furnishes hard copies of the solicitation; in others, the solicitation is made available on the Internet.

EXHIBIT 19-1
The Uniform Contract Format

Part I: The Schedule

A	Solicitation/contract form
B	Supplies or services and price/costs
C	Description/specifications/statement of work
D	Packaging and marking
E	Inspection and acceptance
F	Deliveries or performance
G	Contract administration data
H	Special contract requirements

Part II: Contract Clauses

I	Contract clauses

Part III: List of Documents, Exhibits, Other Attachments

J	List of attachments

Part IV: Representations and Instructions

K	Representations, certifications, and other statements of offerors or respondents
L	Instructions, conditions, and notices to offerors or respondents
M	Evaluation factors for award

EXHIBIT 19-2
Instructions to Offerors—Competitive Acquisition
(FAR 52.215-1, January 2004)

(a) *Definitions.* As used in this provision—

"Discussions" are negotiations that occur after establishment of the competitive range that may, at the Contracting Officer's discretion, result in the offeror being allowed to revise its proposal.

"In writing," "writing," or "written" means any worded or numbered expression that can be read, reproduced, and later communicated, and includes electronically transmitted and stored information.

"Proposal modification" is a change made to a proposal before the solicitation's closing date and time, or made in response to an amendment, or made to correct a mistake at any time before award.

"Proposal revision" is a change to a proposal made after the solicitation closing date, at the request of or as allowed by a Contracting Officer as the result of negotiations.

"Time," if stated as a number of days, is calculated using calendar days, unless otherwise specified, and will include Saturdays, Sundays, and legal holidays. However, if the last day falls on a Saturday, Sunday, or legal holiday, then the period shall include the next working day.

(b) *Amendments to solicitations.* If this solicitation is amended, all terms and conditions that are not amended remain unchanged. Offerors shall acknowledge receipt of any amendment to this solicitation by the date and time specified in the amendment(s).

(c) *Submission, modification, revision, and withdrawal of proposals.*

(1) Unless other methods (e.g., electronic commerce or facsimile) are permitted in the solicitation, proposals and modifications to proposals shall be submitted in paper media in sealed envelopes or packages (i) addressed to the office specified in the solicitation, and (ii) showing the time and date specified for receipt, the solicitation number, and the name and address of the offeror. Offerors using commercial carriers should ensure that the proposal is marked on the outermost wrapper with the information in paragraphs (c)(1)(i) and (c)(1)(ii) of this provision.

(2) The first page of the proposal must show—
  (i) The solicitation number;
  (ii) The name, address, and telephone and facsimile numbers of the offeror (and electronic address if available);

(iii) A statement specifying the extent of agreement with all terms, conditions, and provisions included in the solicitation and agreement to furnish any or all items upon which prices are offered at the price set opposite each item;

(iv) Names, titles, and telephone and facsimile numbers (and electronic addresses if available) of persons authorized to negotiate on the offeror's behalf with the Government in connection with this solicitation; and

(v) Name, title, and signature of person authorized to sign the proposal. Proposals signed by an agent shall be accompanied by evidence of that agent's authority, unless that evidence has been previously furnished to the issuing office.

(3) Submission, modification, revision, and withdrawal of proposals.

    (i) Offerors are responsible for submitting proposals, and any modifications or revisions, so as to reach the Government office designated in the solicitation by the time specified in the solicitation. If no time is specified in the solicitation, the time for receipt is 4:30 p.m., local time, for the designated Government office on the date that proposal or revision is due.

    (ii) (A) Any proposal, modification, or revision received at the Government office designated in the solicitation after the exact time specified for receipt of offers is "late" and will not be considered unless it is received before award is made, the Contracting Officer determines that accepting the late offer would not unduly delay the acquisition; and—

        (1) If it was transmitted through an electronic commerce method authorized by the solicitation, it was received at the initial point of entry to the Government infrastructure not later than 5:00 p.m. one working day prior to the date specified for receipt of proposals; or

        (2) There is acceptable evidence to establish that it was received at the Government installation designated for receipt of offers and was under the Government's control prior to the time set for receipt of offers; or

        (3) It is the only proposal received.

    (B) However, a late modification of an otherwise successful proposal that makes its terms more favorable to the Government, will be considered at any time it is received and may be accepted.

(iii) Acceptable evidence to establish the time of receipt at the Government installation includes the time/date stamp of that installation on the proposal wrapper, other documentary evidence of receipt maintained by the installation, or oral testimony or statements of Government personnel.

(iv) If an emergency or unanticipated event interrupts normal Government processes so that proposals cannot be received at the office designated for receipt of proposals by the exact time specified in the solicitation, and urgent Government requirements preclude amendment of the solicitation, the time specified for receipt of proposals will be deemed to be extended to the same time of day specified in the solicitation on the first work day on which normal Government processes resume.

(v) Proposals may be withdrawn by written notice received at any time before award. Oral proposals in response to oral solicitations may be withdrawn orally. If the solicitation authorizes facsimile proposals, proposals may be withdrawn via facsimile received at any time before award, subject to the conditions specified in the provision at 52.215-5 Facsimile Proposals. Proposals may be withdrawn in person by an offeror or an authorized representative, if the identity of the person requesting withdrawal is established and the person signs a receipt for the proposal before award.

(4) Unless otherwise specified in the solicitation, the offeror may propose to provide any item or combination of items.

(5) Offerors shall submit proposals in response to this solicitation in English, unless otherwise permitted by the solicitation, and in U.S. dollars, unless the provision at FAR 52.225-17, Evaluation of Foreign Currency Offers, is included in the solicitation.

(6) Offerors may submit modifications to their proposals at any time before the solicitation closing date and time, and may submit modifications in response to an amendment, or to correct a mistake at any time before award.

(7) Offerors may submit revised proposals only if requested or allowed by the Contracting Officer.

(8) Proposals may be withdrawn at any time before award. Withdrawals are effective upon receipt of notice by the Contracting Officer.

(d) *Offer expiration date.* Proposals in response to this solicitation will be valid for the number of days specified on the solicitation cover sheet (unless a different period is proposed by the offeror).

(e) *Restriction on disclosure and use of data*. Offerors that include in their proposals data that they do not want disclosed to the public for any purpose, or used by the Government except for evaluation purposes, shall—

(1) Mark the title page with the following legend:

This proposal includes data that shall not be disclosed outside the Government and shall not be duplicated, used, or disclosed—in whole or in part—for any purpose other than to evaluate this proposal. If, however, a contract is awarded to this offeror as a result of—or in connection with—the submission of this data, the Government shall have the right to duplicate, use, or disclose the data to the extent provided in the resulting contract. This restriction does not limit the Government's right to use information contained in this data if it is obtained from another source without restriction. The data subject to this restriction are contained in sheets [*insert numbers or other identification of sheets*]; and

(2) Mark each sheet of data it wishes to restrict with the following legend:

Use or disclosure of data contained on this sheet is subject to the restriction on the title page of this proposal.

(f) *Contract award.*

(1) The Government intends to award a contract or contracts resulting from this solicitation to the responsible offeror(s) whose proposal(s) represents the best value after evaluation in accordance with the factors and subfactors in the solicitation.

(2) The Government may reject any or all proposals if such action is in the Government's interest.

(3) The Government may waive informalities and minor irregularities in proposals received.

(4) The Government intends to evaluate proposals and award a contract without discussions with offerors (except clarifications as described in FAR 15.306(a)). Therefore, the offeror's initial proposal should contain the offeror's best terms from a cost or price and technical standpoint. The Government reserves the right to conduct discussions if the Contracting Officer later determines them to be necessary. If the Contracting Officer determines that the number of proposals that would otherwise be in the competitive range exceeds the number at which an efficient competition can be conducted, the Contracting Officer may limit the number of proposals in the competitive range to the greatest number that will permit an efficient competition among the most highly rated proposals.

(5) The Government reserves the right to make an award on any item for a quantity less than the quantity offered, at the unit cost or prices offered, unless the offeror specifies otherwise in the proposal.

(6) The Government reserves the right to make multiple awards if, after considering the additional administrative costs, it is in the Government's best interest to do so.

(7) Exchanges with offerors after receipt of a proposal do not constitute a rejection or counteroffer by the Government.

(8) The Government may determine that a proposal is unacceptable if the prices proposed are materially unbalanced between line items or subline items. Unbalanced pricing exists when, despite an acceptable total evaluated price, the price of one or more contract line items is significantly overstated or understated as indicated by the application of cost or price analysis techniques. A proposal may be rejected if the Contracting Officer determines that the lack of balance poses an unacceptable risk to the Government.

(9) If a cost realism analysis is performed, cost realism may be considered by the source selection authority in evaluating performance or schedule risk.

(10) A written award or acceptance of proposal mailed or otherwise furnished to the successful offeror within the time specified in the proposal shall result in a binding contract without further action by either party.

(11) If a post-award debriefing is given to requesting offerors, the Government shall disclose the following information, if applicable:

    (i) The agency's evaluation of the significant weak or deficient factors in the debriefed offeror's offer.

    (ii) The overall evaluated cost or price and technical rating of the successful and the debriefed offeror and past performance information on the debriefed offeror.

    (iii) The overall ranking of all offerors, when any ranking was developed by the agency during source selection.

    (iv) A summary of the rationale for award.

    (v) For acquisitions of commercial items, the make and model of the item to be delivered by the successful offeror.

    (vi) Reasonable responses to relevant questions posed by the debriefed offeror as to whether source-selection procedures set forth in the solicitation, applicable regulations, and other applicable authorities were followed by the agency.

(End of provision)

Alternate I (Oct 1997). As prescribed in 15.209(a)(1), substitute the following paragraph (f)(4) for paragraph (f)(4) of the basic provision:

> (f)(4) The Government intends to evaluate proposals and award a contract after conducting discussions with offerors whose proposals have been determined to be within the competitive range. If the Contracting Officer determines that the number of proposals that would otherwise be in the competitive range exceeds the number at which an efficient competition can be conducted, the Contracting Officer may limit the number of proposals in the competitive range to the greatest number that will permit an efficient competition among the most highly rated proposals. Therefore, the offeror's initial proposal should contain the offeror's best terms from a price and technical standpoint.

Alternate II (Oct 1997). As prescribed in 15.209 (a)(2), add a paragraph (c)(9) substantially the same as the following to the basic clause:

> (c)(9) Offerors may submit proposals that depart from stated requirements. Such proposals shall clearly identify why the acceptance of the proposal would be advantageous to the Government. Any deviations from the terms and conditions of the solicitation, as well as the comparative advantage to the Government, shall be clearly identified and explicitly defined. The Government reserves the right to amend the solicitation to allow all offerors an opportunity to submit revised proposals based on the revised requirements.

(1) If this contract is completely or partially terminated, the Contractor shall make available the records relating to the work terminated until 3 years after any resulting final termination settlement; and

(2) The Contractor shall make available records relating to appeals under the Disputes clause or to litigation or the settlement of claims arising under or relating to this contract until such appeals, litigation, or claims are finally resolved.

Chapter 20

HOLDING A PREPROPOSAL CONFERENCE

A preproposal conference is a meeting held so that the government and potential offerors can jointly review the content of the solicitation before proposals are submitted. This can greatly reduce the risk of misinterpretation and subsequent problems in the source selection process.

NOTIFYING CONTRACTORS OF A CONFERENCE

Contractors can be invited to a preproposal conference in the initial solicitation, in an amendment to the solicitation, or by letter. An announcement of the preproposal conference can also be posted at the GPE.

LACK OF FAR GUIDANCE

The FAR once contained more detailed coverage on the conduct of preproposal meetings but now only mentions them briefly at 15.201, under the general heading "Exchanges with industry before receipt of proposals."

The more detailed FAR coverage was sound advice. For that reason, we quote it here:

(a) A preproposal conference may be held to brief prospective offerors after a solicitation has been issued but before offers are submitted. Generally, the Government uses these conferences in complex negotiated acquisitions to explain or clarify complicated specifications and requirements.

(b) The contracting officer shall decide if a preproposal conference is required and make the necessary arrangements, including the following:

(1) If notice was not in the solicitation, give all prospective offerors who received the solicitation adequate notice of the time, place, nature, and scope of the conference.

(2) If time allows, request prospective offerors to submit written questions in advance. Prepared answers can then be delivered during the conference.

(3) Arrange for technical and legal personnel to attend the conference, if appropriate.

(c) The contracting officer or a designated representative shall conduct the preproposal conference, furnish all prospective offerors identical information concerning the proposed acquisition, make a complete record of the conference, and promptly furnish a copy of that record to all prospective offerors. Conferees shall be advised that—

(1) Remarks and explanations at the conference shall not qualify the terms of the solicitation; and

(2) Terms of the solicitation and specifications remain unchanged unless the solicitation is amended in writing.

SITE VISITS

When the work to be required under a contract will include work done at a government location, it is common to invite potential offerors to visit the work site. A site visit can be considered a preproposal conference whenever questions are asked and answers given. Sometimes the government makes such site visits mandatory.

AGENCY PRACTICES

Often the government follows up a preproposal conference by issuing a solicitation amendment that sets forth all of the questions asked and the answers given at the conference. Some agencies have their own written procedures and policies specifically addressing preproposal conferences; others do not.

Manager Alert
While the term *preproposal conference* has traditionally been used for conferences held after the solicitation has been issued, some agencies (such as NASA) may use the term to describe meetings held after a draft request for proposals (RFP) is issued but before the actual RFP is issued.

PREPROPOSAL CONFERENCE TASK LIST

Exhibit 20-1 shows a checklist used by the National Institute of Allergy and Infectious Diseases for its preproposal conferences. It identifies administrative and other details that should be addressed before, during, and after the conference. The bulk of responsibility rests on the contract specialist, but he or she is required to coordinate frequently with project officers.

EXHIBIT 20-1
Preproposal Conference Checklist

General Guidelines
- ✓ Work with project officers to determine whether to limit the number of people from each company.
- ✓ Work with project officers to determine whether to allow personal recording devices, cameras, or video equipment.
- ✓ Work with project officers to decide whether to create a reading room where offerors can review documentation.
- ✓ Post the date, time, and location to give offerors enough time to read the RFP, prepare for the conference, and make travel arrangements.
- ✓ Notify offerors they will need a picture identification to enter the facility.
- ✓ Post the following disclaimer when inviting offerors or read it at the conference.

    "A preproposal conference is for informational purposes only. It may answer some offeror questions; NIAID posts all questions at_____. Statements or representations made during the conference are not legally binding. Changes resulting from the conference are official only if issued through an amendment to the RFP."

Attendance Requests
- ✓ If reservations are needed due to anticipated size of the meeting, create a cutoff date for attendance requests.
- ✓ Send offerors an email address or fax number to submit their requests.
- ✓ Determine whether to post the attendance list or otherwise make it available to potential offerors.
- ✓ Notify offerors if releasing their name or company.

Preparation
- ✓ Reserve a meeting room large enough for group and accessible to handicapped persons.
- ✓ Work with project officers to identify conference presenters.
- ✓ Work with project officers to identify needed technical resources.
- ✓ Work with project officers to prepare an agenda.
- ✓ Prepare extra copies of the RFP and amendments for the conference. Make sure all materials are posted for the general population; see FAR 15.201.

- ✓ Ensure the conference is recorded or a transcript is made.
- ✓ Prepare a registration signup sheet.

Conducting a Preproposal Conference
- ✓ Initiate the recording by noting the date, time, RFP number, and project title.
- ✓ Welcome participants and introduce key people.
- ✓ Remind participants they must sign the registration sheet.
- ✓ Explain the purpose of the conference and how it will be conducted.
- ✓ Ask attendees to state their name and organization before asking questions, for recording purposes.
- ✓ Reread the disclaimer stated above.
- ✓ Work through the prepared agenda.

After a Preproposal Conference
- ✓ Review the transcript or recording of the conference to determine if an amendment to the RFP is required.
- ✓ Post all questions and answers.
- ✓ Post a register of attendees.

(Source: National Institute of Allergy and Infectious Diseases. Available at www.niaid.nih.gov/researchfunding/tool/pages/preproconf.aspx. Accessed October 2012)

Chapter 21

BRIEFING EVALUATORS AND ADVISORS

It is standard practice to brief evaluators and advisory groups before the government receives proposals. The source selection authority controls the briefing, which is usually given by the contracting officer or his or her representative, such as a contract specialist. Legal counsel and senior program officials also may participate in the briefing.

A briefing should include:

- Reiteration of the rules for protecting sensitive procurement information, including a discussion of the Procurement Integrity Act
- Emphasizing that any contact with competing contractors must be authorized or directed by the contracting officer.
- Discussion of conflict of interest rules and related matters, including offers of employment
- Examination and discussion of the requirements document
- Examination and discussion of the proposal preparation instructions
- Examination and discussion of the evaluation factors
- An explanation of the evaluation process to be used, including examination of the rating methodology and the scoring/rating categories to be used
- Discussion of the lines of communication in the source selection organization structure
- Informing evaluators that their job is to evaluate the proposals against the criteria in the solicitation, not against each other
- Explanation of the FAR requirement that the relative strengths, deficiencies, significant weaknesses, and risks supporting proposal evaluation be documented in the contract file

- Definition of *strengths, deficiencies, significant weaknesses, weaknesses, risk, clarifications, communications,* and *meaningful discussions*
- A review of individual evaluation forms (an example form for a trade-off procurement appears as Exhibit 21-1)
- A review of summary evaluation forms
- If an SSAC or other advisors are to be used, discussion of the role these advisors will play in the process
- If nongovernment personnel are to be used as evaluators or advisors, discussion of the role they will play in the process and an explanation of limits on the material/information to which they will have access
- A review of established milestones for the remainder of the source selection process
- Questions and answers.

Some agencies may use pre–source selection instructional booklets, tapes, CDs, DVDs, or other media to supplement the briefing process.

> **Manager Alert**
> A thorough, high-quality evaluator briefing helps to get everyone on the same page and strengthens protection against potentially grievous errors (i.e., mistakes that could delay the process, precipitate protests, or abort the acquisition).

EXHIBIT 21-1
Sample Evaluation Form for a Trade-off Procurement

Proposal _____

Evaluation factor _____

Evaluator _____

Score/rating _____

Note: Evaluator should attach continuation sheets as needed.

Strengths/benefits

_____
_____
_____
_____
_____

Clarifications/explanations needed

_____
_____
_____
_____
_____

Deficiencies

_____
_____
_____
_____
_____

Significant weaknesses

_____
_____
_____
_____
_____
_____
_____
_____

Weaknesses

_____
_____
_____
_____
_____
_____
_____

Comments/rationale

_____
_____
_____
_____
_____
_____
_____
_____

Signed_____ Date _____

Source: Reprinted with permission of SciTech Services Inc., Edgewood, MD.

Chapter 22

EVALUATING MERIT/ TECHNICAL FACTORS

For some acquisitions, a single team, often called a technical evaluation team or some similar name, evaluates all non-cost factors. For others, there may be individual teams for the various evaluation factors. For example, one team may evaluate technical approach, another management considerations, another past performance, and so on. The steps described in this chapter apply to either of those approaches.

BEGINNING PROPOSAL EVALUATIONS

The evaluation of proposals begins after the closing date for receipt of proposals. At that time, the contracting officer distributes copies of the proposals to the chair of the evaluation team or teams.

This distribution often takes place after contracting personnel do an initial screening to ascertain if contractors followed the government's instructions regarding media, content, format, and length. Noncompliant proposals are identified for the contracting officer so that he or she can take appropriate action. He or she may, for example, determine that the offeror is not responsive and eliminate the offeror from the competition.

A TYPICAL EVALUATION PROCESS

Following distribution of proposals, a typical evaluation process might go as follows:
1. The chairperson of the evaluation team convenes a meeting and distributes the relevant portions of the proposal and pertinent evaluation forms to team members. This meeting may also include a review of information given in earlier briefings on the duties and responsibilities of

evaluators. If such briefings have not yet been given, the evaluation team chair advises evaluators of all of the elements discussed in Chapter 21.

2. If offerors are to give oral presentations, the schedule for the presentations and pertinent evaluation forms are distributed to evaluators.

3. The evaluation methodology is reviewed in detail so that all evaluators have a common understanding of the characteristics a proposal should have to earn a specific rating for an evaluation factor or subfactor. (If it is a lowest cost, technically acceptable [LPTA] acquisition, the only possible rating is "acceptable" or "not acceptable.")

4. Each team member evaluates the relevant assigned portions of the written proposals and prepares an evaluation form. Typically, the evaluator will read the assigned material through and then reread before determining a rating or score. This helps prevent evaluators from jumping to erroneous conclusions before reading and understanding all of the proposal content.

5. For oral presentations, evaluators normally document evaluations, using the relevant agency forms, immediately after the presentation. Sometimes, evaluators wait until all presentations are completed before assigning ratings. In those cases, the evaluators often review electronic recordings of the presentations or written records rather than just relying on memory and notes.

6. If it is an LPTA acquisition, the evaluation documentation must indicate whether the proposal was acceptable or not acceptable for each factor being evaluated. Evaluators must provide supporting rationale for their findings. If the proposal is rated "not acceptable" on one or more factors, the supporting rationale must clearly identify the deficiencies, significant weaknesses, or both that resulted in that finding. It is not necessary to address the strengths of the proposal, except perhaps to justify a finding of acceptability, since the relative strengths of acceptable proposals are not a factor in the selection.

7. In a trade-off acquisition, the evaluator determines a rating or score for each assigned evaluation factor, along with supporting rationale. FAR 15.305 specifically requires, at a minimum, "an assessment of each offeror's ability to accomplish the technical requirements." Unlike an LPTA acquisition, "proposals may be evaluated to distinguish their relative quality by considering the degree to which they exceed the minimum requirements or will better satisfy the agency's needs" (ViroMed Laboratories Inc., B-310747.4, January 22, 2009).

8. In the event award is to be made without discussions, the evaluators must indicate any proposal areas where clarifications from competing contractors are needed or desired before a finding regarding acceptability

Chapter 22

EVALUATING MERIT/ TECHNICAL FACTORS

For some acquisitions, a single team, often called a technical evaluation team or some similar name, evaluates all non-cost factors. For others, there may be individual teams for the various evaluation factors. For example, one team may evaluate technical approach, another management considerations, another past performance, and so on. The steps described in this chapter apply to either of those approaches.

BEGINNING PROPOSAL EVALUATIONS

The evaluation of proposals begins after the closing date for receipt of proposals. At that time, the contracting officer distributes copies of the proposals to the chair of the evaluation team or teams.

This distribution often takes place after contracting personnel do an initial screening to ascertain if contractors followed the government's instructions regarding media, content, format, and length. Noncompliant proposals are identified for the contracting officer so that he or she can take appropriate action. He or she may, for example, determine that the offeror is not responsive and eliminate the offeror from the competition.

A TYPICAL EVALUATION PROCESS

Following distribution of proposals, a typical evaluation process might go as follows:
1. The chairperson of the evaluation team convenes a meeting and distributes the relevant portions of the proposal and pertinent evaluation forms to team members. This meeting may also include a review of information given in earlier briefings on the duties and responsibilities of

evaluators. If such briefings have not yet been given, the evaluation team chair advises evaluators of all of the elements discussed in Chapter 21.

2. If offerors are to give oral presentations, the schedule for the presentations and pertinent evaluation forms are distributed to evaluators.

3. The evaluation methodology is reviewed in detail so that all evaluators have a common understanding of the characteristics a proposal should have to earn a specific rating for an evaluation factor or subfactor. (If it is a lowest cost, technically acceptable [LPTA] acquisition, the only possible rating is "acceptable" or "not acceptable.")

4. Each team member evaluates the relevant assigned portions of the written proposals and prepares an evaluation form. Typically, the evaluator will read the assigned material through and then reread before determining a rating or score. This helps prevent evaluators from jumping to erroneous conclusions before reading and understanding all of the proposal content.

5. For oral presentations, evaluators normally document evaluations, using the relevant agency forms, immediately after the presentation. Sometimes, evaluators wait until all presentations are completed before assigning ratings. In those cases, the evaluators often review electronic recordings of the presentations or written records rather than just relying on memory and notes.

6. If it is an LPTA acquisition, the evaluation documentation must indicate whether the proposal was acceptable or not acceptable for each factor being evaluated. Evaluators must provide supporting rationale for their findings. If the proposal is rated "not acceptable" on one or more factors, the supporting rationale must clearly identify the deficiencies, significant weaknesses, or both that resulted in that finding. It is not necessary to address the strengths of the proposal, except perhaps to justify a finding of acceptability, since the relative strengths of acceptable proposals are not a factor in the selection.

7. In a trade-off acquisition, the evaluator determines a rating or score for each assigned evaluation factor, along with supporting rationale. FAR 15.305 specifically requires, at a minimum, "an assessment of each offeror's ability to accomplish the technical requirements." Unlike an LPTA acquisition, "proposals may be evaluated to distinguish their relative quality by considering the degree to which they exceed the minimum requirements or will better satisfy the agency's needs" (ViroMed Laboratories Inc., B-310747.4, January 22, 2009).

8. In the event award is to be made without discussions, the evaluators must indicate any proposal areas where clarifications from competing contractors are needed or desired before a finding regarding acceptability

Chapter 22: Evaluating Merit/Technical Factors 101

is made or a trade-off score is assigned. The exchange that the FAR calls *clarifications* applies only to situations where award is to be made without discussions.

9. The team meets at the call of the chairperson and attempts to reach a consensus on scores and/or findings so that a summary report can be sent to the contracting officer and source selection authority (SSA). In more complex procurements, this report is submitted to the SSA through a source selection evaluation board chairperson (who oversees the functioning of the individual evaluation teams) and/or a source selection advisory council, and perhaps through other designated advisory persons or groups.

10. In the event evaluators cannot reach a consensus opinion, some agencies forward both a majority report and a minority report. Others use some sort of averaging or middle ground, take a majority-rules vote, or rely on the chairperson to make a final decision. It is recommended that a procedure that gives voice to minority opinions be used. It is a dangerous practice to hide disagreement from the contracting officer and/or other SSA by taking an average or a majority-rules approach.

11. When award is to be made without discussions, the summary report and/or advisory reports submitted to the source selection authority identify the strengths and shortcomings of proposals and may contain a recommendation for award. Some agencies require such a recommendation, others prohibit it, and still others leave the matter to the wishes of the particular contracting officer or SSA. No recommendation for award is necessary for LPTA acquisitions, because award will go to the lowest price among acceptable proposals.

12. When a competitive range is to be established, the report indicates whether, in the view of evaluators, there is any need for communications before the competitive range is established. (The exchange called *communications* is used only when a competitive range is to be established and discussions are to be held.) Some agencies require or request recommendations in the summary report as to which contractors should be included in the competitive range, whereas others do not.

13. If communications or clarifications occur, proposals are reevaluated, and changes may be made to the summary report as appropriate. (Note that in some situations, the contracting officer is notified of the need for communications or clarifications before a summary report is prepared. In such cases, only a single summary report is prepared after communications or clarifications are held.)

14. Once the competitive range has been established, evaluators may be asked to assist the contracting officer in preparing for discussions with those in the competitive range. If written discussions are planned,

evaluators may be asked to participate in preparing the letters to the competing contractors that have been placed in the competitive range. If oral discussions are to take place, evaluators may be asked to help prepare a negotiation plan, to participate in the discussions, or to do both.

15. Following completion of discussions and the receipt of final proposal revisions, evaluators reevaluate the proposals in the competitive range and send a new summary report to the source selection authority. The summary report may or may not include a recommendation for award, depending upon agency practices. The SSA then prepares the appropriate selection document and selects the source.

USE OF AGENCY FORMS

Some agencies (the U.S. Army, for example) include in their evaluation and summary report forms an Item for Negotiation form, which can be used to document matters that must be clarified, communicated, or discussed. Other agencies have automated systems in which evaluation data can be entered as appropriate and then arrayed in a user-friendly fashion. Use of these automated systems does not alter the basic rules of source selection.

MATCHING THE WORDS WITH THE MUSIC

It is the responsibility of the contracting officer and the SSA to review evaluation reports carefully to look for errors, omissions, or anomalies. Too frequently, these officials receive a report in which the words do not match the music. For example, a report might show that a proposal has been given an outstanding rating, but there is a relatively long list of deficiencies and weaknesses. Or, conversely, a proposal might receive a lesser rating, but there are no listed deficiencies or weaknesses.

RETAINING EVALUATORS AND RETAINING EVALUATION FORMS

Competent, consistent, and unbiased evaluation of meaningful evaluation factors is critical to the source selection process. Whenever possible, the same evaluators should be used throughout the process.

It is normal practice for most agencies to retain individual evaluator rating forms even after summary reports are prepared. However, those that do not retain them are apparently on safe ground, provided that final documentation can reasonably demonstrate the bases upon which the judgments were made. In Government Acquisitions Inc., B-401048, May 4, 2009, the comptroller general opined:

Although an agency must document its evaluation judgments in sufficient detail to show that they are not arbitrary, the necessary amount and level of detail will vary from procurement to procurement. U.S. Defense Sys., Inc., B-245563, Jan. 17, 1992, 92-1 CPD para. 89 at 3; Champion-Alliance, Inc., B-249504, Dec. 1, 1992, 92-2 CPD para. 386 at 6-7. For example, there is no requirement that the evaluation record must include narrative explanations for every rating assigned. Apex Marine Ship Mgmt. Co., LLC; American V-Ships Marine, Ltd., B-278276.25, B-278276.28, Sept. 25, 2000, 2000 CPD para. 164 at 8-9. Similarly, there is no requirement that an agency retain individual evaluators' notes or worksheets, provided the agency's final evaluation documentation reasonably explains the basis for the agency's judgments.

EVALUATING SMALL BUSINESS SUBCONTRACTING PLANS

One part of non-cost evaluation that is usually done separately from the evaluation of other merit factors is the evaluation of small business subcontracting plans. FAR 19.705-4 and the solicitation provision at FAR 52.219-9 give the contracting officer the responsibility for determining the adequacy of submitted plans. Normally, the contracting officer asks agency small business advisors and the program office responsible for the requirement being procured for assistance or guidance in evaluating these plans.

Manager Alert

Although the statutorily independent SSA does not have to agree with or even comply with the evaluator findings, he or she must consider them. However, notwithstanding this independence, it is clear that the SSA normally does rely a great deal on the opinions and expertise of evaluators. If the evaluators do not do their jobs properly, all of the careful planning and hard work expended to this point might be for naught. Proposal evaluation is truly "where the rubber meets the road" in the source selection process.

Chapter 23

EVALUATING PAST PERFORMANCE

In evaluating past performance, members of the evaluation team, often a separate performance risk assessment group, have some specific FAR guidance to take into account. FAR 15.305 requires the following:

- The government shall consider information obtained from an offeror, as well as information obtained from any other sources, when evaluating the offeror's past performance.
- The contracting officer/source selection authority (SSA) shall determine the relevance of past performance information.
- The evaluation should take into account past performance information regarding predecessor companies, key personnel who have relevant experience, or subcontractors that will perform major or critical aspects of the requirement when such information is relevant to the instant acquisition.
- If the case of an offeror that does not have a record of relevant past performance, or for whom information on past performance is not available, the offeror may not be evaluated favorably or unfavorably on past performance.
- The evaluation should include the past performance of offerors in complying with subcontracting plan goals for small disadvantaged business concerns.

Often, past performance evaluators conduct telephone interviews with the customers identified by contractors in their proposals or otherwise known to the government and may use standardized questionnaire forms developed by their agency. They also search the Past Performance Information Retrieval System and any other available government databases for relevant data. If additional information is needed, evaluators may gather it from external sources such as the Better Business Bureau.

One rather tricky part of the FAR guidance on evaluating past performance concerns the relevance of a competing contractor's past performance and/or the relevance of information on predecessor companies, key personnel, and subcontractors. Because it is the source selection authority who must determine the relevance of this past performance information, it may be necessary for the evaluation group to communicate with the source selection authority during the evaluation process. Alternatively, the evaluation group could include all past performance information in its report and allow for the source selection authority to make his or her determination of relevancy after evaluations are complete. The evaluation group may or may not make a recommendation regarding relevancy, depending on the rules of the agency, the wishes of the source selection authority, or both.

WHEN THERE IS NO PAST PERFORMANCE INFORMATION

The most controversial part of the FAR guidance on past performance concerns competing contractors that have no discernible relevant past performance. They are to be treated neither favorably nor unfavorably. (Earlier FAR coverage had indicated that competing contractors without past performance must be given a neutral evaluation.) There was, and to some extent still is, confusion as to exactly how this should be accomplished.

Those who publish the FAR apparently hoped to minimize the use of the neutral rating (a rating that is neither favorable nor unfavorable) by opening the door to consideration of predecessor companies, key personnel, and subcontractors when a competing contractor has no relevant past performance. Nonetheless, agencies still encounter numerous situations where an offeror lacks relevant past performance.

The two most common methods of evaluation when there is a lack of relevant past performance data seem to be a technique called *splitting the difference* and a technique in which past performance is not considered at all in the determination of final evaluation ratings.

To illustrate the first method, presume that a competing contractor could get up to 5 points for exceptional performance and as few as 0 points for poor past performance. A competing contractor with no past performance would get 2.5 points. While it may seem that this score is not compatible with a literal reading of the FAR guidance (because it is unfavorable with respect to excellent performers, and favorable with respect to poor performers), splitting the difference has been upheld by the comptroller general and has been used by a number of agencies.

To illustrate the second method, presume that a solicitation called for the evaluation of proposals based on technical merit, past performance, and cost. Also presume that there were a number of competing contractors and that one of them had no relevant past performance. In determining the competitive range, the contracting officer would identify the highest rated of the offerors being evaluated on all three factors. Then past performance would be removed as an evaluation factor when comparing these contractors against the competing contractor with no past performance before determining a competitive range. The same technique would be used in establishing final ratings prior to the source selection decision. In that case, the SSA would select the best value among competing contractors with past performance. He or she would then remove past performance as an evaluation factor and compare the tentative best value against the competing contractor that lacked relevant past performance before making the final source selection.

> **Manager Alert**
>
> The comptroller general has held in protest opinions that, notwithstanding a literal interpretation of the FAR, a source selection authority may consider a contractor with a good record of past performance to be more attractive than a contractor with no past performance. In Phillips Industries, Inc., B-280645, September 17, 1998, the comptroller general opined:
>
>> The use of a neutral rating approach, to avoid penalizing a vendor without prior experience and thereby enhance competition, does not preclude, in a best value procurement, a determination to award to a higher-priced offeror with a good past performance record over a lower-cost vendor with a neutral past performance rating. Indeed such a determination is inherent in the concept of best value.
>
> Past performance evaluation forms, including any recommendations given by evaluators, can best serve the contracting officer and source selection authority if they indicate specifically how any lack of past performance does or does not contribute to the risk of successful contract performance. This information can be invaluable in making, documenting, and defending the source selection decision.

OTHER PAST PERFORMANCE EVALUATOR RESPONSIBILITIES

Past performance evaluators must also point out situations where clarifications or communications are desired or required regarding past performance. And they must properly categorize each contractor—for example, as high risk, low risk, moderate risk, and so on—and furnish the source selection authority with supporting rationale. As is true for other evaluation factors, differences of evaluator opinion may arise requiring meetings and the development, where feasible, of consensus opinions.

Chapter 24

EVALUATING PROPOSED COST OR PRICE

While technical evaluators are assessing the non-cost portions of proposals, the contracting officer or other source selection authority (SSA) obtains evaluations of the price or cost proposals. Cost or price evaluations may be performed by an individual or by a group such as a separate cost evaluation team.

Agencies perform either price analysis or cost analysis when evaluating proposals. Price analysis is the less labor-intensive of these approaches since it merely requires comparing the price offered to various yardsticks, such as other prices received and/or the government's estimate. Cost analysis, on the other hand, requires a line-by-line examination of the cost elements that make up a proposed total cost or price. These may include labor, material, subcontracting, indirect costs, and profit or fee. The object of both kinds of analyses is to award a contract with a cost or price that is fair and reasonable.

FAR PREFERENCE

The FAR establishes a preference for price analysis when it indicates that cost analysis will be used in "limited situations." FAR 15.305(a)(1) provides the following:

> *Cost or price evaluation.* Normally, competition establishes price reasonableness. Therefore, when contracting on a firm-fixed-price or fixed-price with economic price adjustment basis, comparison of the proposed prices will usually satisfy the requirement to perform a price analysis, and a cost analysis need not be performed. In limited situations, a cost analysis . . . may be appropriate to establish reasonableness of the otherwise successful offeror's price. When contracting on a cost-reimbursement basis, evaluations shall include a cost realism analysis to determine what the Government should realistically expect to pay for the proposed effort, the offeror's understanding of the work, and the offeror's ability to perform the contract. (See 37.115 for uncompensated overtime evaluation.) The contracting officer shall document the cost or price evaluation.

WHEN COST ANALYSIS IS ESSENTIAL

Despite the FAR preference for price analysis, many situations exist where some sort of cost analysis is essential. These include situations where technical factors are important to the selection decision and costs can vary depending on the quality and the approach of the proposal. For example, a reasonable cost for one technical approach may be quite different from a reasonable cost for a competing technical approach. Thus, determining reasonableness through comparison of proposed prices would not pass the common sense test. Cost analysis situations also include those source selections for cost-reimbursement contracts where a cost realism analysis (see below) is required.

Cost analysis may require input from government auditors regarding whether certain proposed costs are allowable under government cost standards, allocable to the contract, and reasonable.

COST REALISM AND PROBABLE COST

FAR 15.404-1(d) defines *cost realism analysis* as "the process of independently reviewing and evaluating specific elements of each offeror's proposed cost estimate to determine whether the estimated proposed cost elements are realistic for the work to be performed; reflect a clear understanding of the requirements; and are consistent with the unique methods of performance and materials described in the offeror's technical proposal."

The FAR requires that cost realism analysis be performed on selections for cost-reimbursement contracts to determine the probable cost of performance. It also requires that the government estimate of the probable cost, rather than the contractor-proposed cost, be used in determining the best value. This makes good business sense for the government because, under cost-reimbursement contracts, the government will ultimately pay the actual allowable costs that were reasonably incurred by the contractor. These actual costs may prove to be quite different from—and are often significantly greater than—proposed costs.

The FAR also permits, but does not require, the use of cost realism analysis on various types of fixed-price contracts. This allows the government to determine if a competing contractor fully understands the requirement and can aid in risk assessments and responsibility determinations.

An Independent Government Cost Estimate for Every Proposal

FAR 15.404-1 (d)(2)(ii) advises that "the probable cost is determined by adjusting each offeror's proposed cost, and fee when appropriate, to reflect any additions or reductions in cost elements to realistic levels based on the results of the cost realism analysis." In essence, this means that the government establishes an independent government cost estimate (IGCE) for each proposal undergoing cost realism analysis.

Wide Variance

Experience has shown that contractors' proposed costs and the government's probable costs can vary considerably and can have a significant impact on the source selection decision. Consider the following contractor-proposed costs and government-estimated probable costs for five proposals in an Army source selection for base operations and support at a Middle East location:

Contractor	Proposed Cost	Probable Cost
A	$226 million	$278 million
B	$173 million	$268 million
C	$135 million	$256 million
D	$270 million	$290 million
E	$189 million	$337 million

The cost evaluation group used an initial IGCE as a baseline and, taking into account each offeror's individual technical approach, adjusted each cost proposal in the areas of staffing levels and labor categories in order to establish the probable cost of each proposal. Despite protests pertaining to the validity of government probable cost estimates, the government's actions were upheld.

Manager Alert

Cost or price evaluators should point out any need for clarifications whenever award is to be made without discussions. If a competitive range is to be established, then the evaluators should identify whether there is a need for communications prior to establishing the competitive range. In no event should cost evaluators contact competing contractors except through, or with the approval of, the contracting officer. The contracting officer is the focal point for any exchanges with competing contractors that occur after the solicitation has been issued.

TECHNICAL ANALYSIS OF COST PROPOSALS

While many cost evaluators are primarily contracting or cost/price experts, there may be a need in specific situations for technical expertise as well. Cost analysis frequently requires judgments about the technical elements of cost proposals, such as the number of labor hours proposed, the categories of labor, the types and quantities of material, tooling, scrap rates, and other cost evaluation matters that require some degree of technical expertise. In some cases, especially those involving "other than formal" selection procedures, technical experts who participated in the evaluation of technical/merit factors will be asked to perform a technical analysis of the cost proposals after their initial evaluation of non-cost factors has been completed.

THE COST EVALUATION REPORT

Following their evaluation of cost proposals, including consideration of any need for clarifications or communications, evaluators submit a report to the contracting officer and SSA. Like the evaluation report for the non-cost factors, the cost evaluation report may be submitted through a source selection evaluation board chairperson or any other designated advisory individuals or groups. The report must identify any questionable areas in proposed cost and, where appropriate, the results of cost realism analyses.

Often this report is combined with the summary report of non-cost factors before it is submitted to the contracting officer and SSA. When award is to be made without discussions, the individual reports (on non-cost factors and cost) or a combined technical/cost report should give the contracting officer and SSA the information needed to make a selection decision. The reports may also, depending on agency procedures, include a recommendation for award.

When a competitive range is to be determined, a combined report may give a recommendation for the competitive range, again depending on agency procedures and any direction given by the contracting officer and/or other SSA.

PARTICIPATION IN DISCUSSIONS

When discussions are to be held with those in the competitive range, price/cost evaluators may be asked to help write letters to contractors, to participate in formulating a negotiation plan, and possibly to participate in face-to-face discussions.

After discussions are complete and final proposal revisions have been submitted, cost evaluators may again have to evaluate any changed proposals. Normally, this is done in concert with non-cost evaluators; a single report (with or without a recommendation for award) is submitted through established channels to the contracting officer and/or other SSA.

Chapter 25

CLARIFICATIONS AND AWARD WITHOUT DISCUSSIONS

If the government notified competing contractors in the solicitation that it intended to do so, the government may make award without holding discussions with the competing contractors. The source selection authority takes into consideration evaluator comments, advisor comments, and any evaluator or advisory recommendations before making the source selection decision.

FAR COVERAGE ON CLARIFICATIONS

Even when discussions will not be held, an exchange with contractors is permitted prior to final evaluation and contract award. That exchange is called *clarifications*. FAR Part 15 explains clarifications as follows (15.306):

    (a) Clarifications and award without discussions

        (1) Clarifications are limited exchanges, between the Government and offerors, that may occur when award without discussions is contemplated.

        (2) If award will be made without conducting discussions, offerors may be given the opportunity to clarify certain aspects of proposals (*e.g.*, the relevance of an offeror's past performance information and adverse past performance information to which the offeror has not previously had an opportunity to respond) or to resolve minor or clerical errors.

Fully appreciating this FAR coverage requires a little parsing. First, it says that clarifications are "limited exchanges." This phrasing was presumably intended to end some agencies' practice of giving competing contractors page after page of clarification questions that, based on sheer magnitude alone, looked a lot like discussions. Second, it says that "offerors may be given an opportunity to clarify certain aspects of proposals." "May" means that the contracting officer can choose whether to give offerors this opportunity.

Certain aspects is not defined. That means the contracting officer must decide on a case-by-case basis what constitutes "certain aspects" that need clarification. The only examples of "certain aspects" provided in the FAR are related to past performance, such as the relevance of past performance information and adverse information to which the offeror has not had an opportunity to respond.

Finally, the FAR indicates that clarifications can also be used to correct "minor or clerical errors." Again the contracting officer will have to use judgment to determine if an error is minor or clerical or if it constitutes a deficiency that will require discussions, not clarifications, if it is to be corrected.

Clearly, there is no need at all for clarifications when the proposal being considered has no opportunity for award. For example, it would make no sense to ask for clarifications from a contractor that has proposed the highest price in a lowest price, technically acceptable (LPTA) source selection when there are other acceptable offerors.

> **Manager Alert**
> Although it would appear that offering contractors the chance to clarify certain aspects of their proposals is completely discretionary, the comptroller general has indicated that in the event of a protest, the record will be examined to determine if this discretion has been properly applied. When one contractor complained that the contracting officer should have allowed it to clarify certain adverse past performance information, the comptroller general opined that the contracting officer was not obliged to seek clarification unless there was some reason to doubt the past performance information. The bottom line is that while contracting officers have discretion regarding clarifications, it is not unfettered discretion. The contracting officer must make a judgment call and defend it if necessary.

LPTA CONTRACT AWARDS

In an LPTA source selection, award is made to the lowest-priced responsible and responsive offeror who has been found to be acceptable on all evaluation factors. If an otherwise lowest-priced offeror is not deemed acceptable solely because of a past performance factor, and if that offeror is a small business, the offeror may request a certificate of competency (COC) from the Small Business Administration (SBA). If a COC is issued, the contracting officer will either award to that offeror or appeal the decision through higher levels within the agency and within the SBA. Normally, however, an award is made to the requesting contractor based on the SBA certification.

CHANGING THE AWARD APPROACH

Even if the solicitation provided for award without discussions, the contracting officer can determine that discussions are required. In that case, a competitive range is established, discussions are held, final proposal revisions are obtained, and final evaluations are performed before an award is made. Conditions that might prompt a contracting officer to choose this course of action include cases in which no acceptable proposal was received or where none of the offered costs or prices could be found to be fair and reasonable.

Chapter 26

ESTABLISHING THE COMPETITIVE RANGE

If award will not be made on the basis of initial proposals, the contracting officer and/or other source selection authority establishes a competitive range. This simply means that the government is not required to hold discussions with all of the contractors that have submitted proposals. Instead, the government may limit the number of offerors with whom it will hold discussions to the cream of the crop.

Some contractors refer to the competitive range as the *short list*.

FAR 15.306 provides that, based upon the ratings of each proposal against all evaluation criteria, the contracting officer shall establish a competitive range that consists of the most highly rated proposals. The FAR also allows the contracting officer to further reduce the number of competing contractors in the competitive range when the number of the most highly rated proposals exceeds a number at which an efficient competition can be conducted.

AVOIDING ARBITRARY CUTOFF POINTS

The FAR specifically requires that the evaluation leading to the competitive range be based on the ratings of each proposal against "all evaluation criteria." That means both merit and cost have to be considered in identifying the highest-rated proposals. It has long been held that it is generally an inappropriate practice to establish arbitrary cutoff points for determining the competitive range—for example, determining that an offeror must receive a technical rating of at least 70 out of 100 to get into the competitive range, or determining that a proposed cost of $1 million or more will eliminate an offeror from the competitive range. Establishing such arbitrary cutoff points would preclude the integrated assessment of merit and cost that the FAR requires.

INCLUSION OF UNACCEPTABLE PROPOSALS

Case law has long held that an unacceptable proposal (a proposal with deficiencies) could be kept in the competitive range while an acceptable proposal could be excluded. For example, an otherwise acceptable proposal could be eliminated if, in comparison with other more attractive offers, it had no reasonable opportunity of receiving the contract award, while a proposal that was not immediately acceptable, but that had high potential if it was made acceptable through discussions, could be kept in the competitive range.

Since FAR coverage now provides for a competitive range consisting of only the most highly rated proposals, it would seem that an unacceptable proposal could be kept in the range only if it were deemed to be among the most highly rated.

REDUCTIONS FOR THE SAKE OF EFFICIENCY

FAR 15.306(c)(2) provides that the contracting officer may further reduce the competitive range for the sake of efficiency. While this FAR provision was intended to be applied case by case. It appears that some agencies may have adopted a standard "efficient" number of proposals—three or five, for example.

CHARACTERISTICS OF THE COMPETITIVE RANGE

The competitive range can expand or contract. For example, a competing contractor excluded from the competitive range can protest or complain about the exclusion and, if the contracting officer believes the contractor's position has merit, the contractor can be added to the competitive range. On the other hand, a competing contractor can be removed from the competitive range if discussions held before final proposal revisions reveal that it should no longer be included in the competitive range.

There is no legally established minimum or maximum number of offerors for competitive range determinations. In one case, a contractor complained to the comptroller general that it was eliminated from the competitive range even though it was rated the second best of the proposals received. The agency had established a competitive range of only one offeror, notwithstanding the FAR guidance that uses the plural when it says, at FAR 15.306, "The contracting officer shall establish a competitive range comprised of the most highly rated proposals." After examining the intent of the FAR coverage, the comptroller general opined, "We conclude that . . . Part 15 . . . does not require that agencies retain in the competitive range a proposal that is determined to have no reasonable prospect of award simply to avoid a competitive range of one. We have long held there is nothing inherently improper in a competitive range of one" (SDS Petroleum Products, Inc., B-280430, September 1, 1998).

> **Manager Alert**
> Although the comptroller general finds nothing inherently wrong with a competitive range of one, he has traditionally given such circumstances "increased scrutiny" in the event of a protest.

A SUBJECTIVE DECISION

Just as is the case in many other elements of the source selection process, business decisions regarding the size and composition of the competitive range can be somewhat subjective. Given identical circumstances, different individuals or groups could come to different conclusions about which competing proposals should be placed in the competitive range.

Chapter 27

THE EXCHANGE KNOWN AS COMMUNICATIONS

The contracting officer may hold—and in some cases must hold—exchanges with competing contractors before establishing a competitive range. These exchanges, which are called *communications*, are intended to address issues that should be explored to help determine whether an individual offeror is among the highest-rated competitors and should be placed in the competitive range.

FAR COVERAGE

FAR 15.306 indicates that communications:
- Shall not provide an opportunity for a contractor to revise its proposal
- May be conducted to enhance government understanding of proposals, allow reasonable interpretation of them, or facilitate the evaluation process
- May be held with only those offerors whose inclusion in the competitive range is uncertain, pending the outcome of communications
- Shall be held with offerors whose past performance is the determining factor preventing them from being placed in the competitive range, and must address adverse past performance information to which an offeror has not had an opportunity to respond
- May not constitute discussions (i.e., communications may not provide the opportunity for a contractor to change its proposal).

WHEN COMMUNICATIONS ARE APPROPRIATE

Communications give competing contractors an opportunity to clarify, but not change, certain aspects (such as ambiguities) of their proposals to enhance government understanding of the proposals so that they can be more accurately evaluated.

If a contractor clearly is not going to be in the competitive range, regardless of the outcome of any communications, then communications are not held. Obviously, in such a case, communications would be a waste of time.

If a contractor clearly is going to be in the competitive range regardless of the outcome of any communications, then communications are not held. Any additional information needed from the competing contractor can be obtained when meaningful discussions are later held with those in the competitive range.

Accordingly, communications are held only when they would affect whether a contractor is to be included in the competitive range.

> **Manager Alert**
> Although communications are largely discretionary, it can be assumed that, in the event of a protest, the comptroller general may look to see if that discretion was properly applied.

REQUIRED COMMUNICATIONS

There is one instance when the FAR requires communications. This is when an offeror is being kept out of the competitive range solely because of an adverse past performance report, presumably one to which the offeror has not already had an opportunity to respond.

The emphasis should be placed on the word *solely*. If an offeror's proposal is not highly rated and would not make the competitive range even with an improved past performance rating, then there would be no reason to hold communications with that offeror. Conversely, if an offeror would be in the competitive range regardless of the outcome of communications, then adverse past performance can be addressed when discussions are held with those in the competitive range.

IDENTIFYING THE NEED FOR COMMUNICATIONS

Normally, proposal evaluators inform the contracting officer in their evaluation reports of any perceived need for communications. Evaluator ratings are subsequently adjusted, when appropriate, after communications are held. The competitive range is then established by the contracting officer and/or other source selection authority following consideration of the ratings and comments furnished by evaluators.

Chapter 28

HOLDING DISCUSSIONS

Before we address the topic of discussions, a look at the unique way in which the government uses otherwise common words is in order. We have already noted that what the general public would call *communications* between the government and contractor are called *exchanges* by the government. One such exchange is called *clarifications*, which may occur when the government intends to make award without discussions. However, if a competitive range is to be established, any request for clarification of proposal content is called a *communication*, not a clarification.

FAR COVERAGE OF DISCUSSIONS

After the competitive range has been established, the government must hold discussions with all of the competing contractors in the competitive range. What are discussions? FAR 15.306(d) tells us that:

- Negotiations are exchanges that are undertaken with the intent of allowing an offeror to revise its proposal.
- Negotiations may include bargaining over price and other requirements of the proposed contract.
- When negotiations are conducted in a competitive acquisition, they take place after the establishment of the competitive range and are called *discussions*.
- The primary objective of discussions is to maximize the government's ability to obtain best value, based on the requirement and the evaluation factors set forth in the solicitation.

Thus, it is clear, and a little amusing, that any discussions held in a noncompetitive environment are called *negotiations*, while any negotiations held in a competitive environment are called *discussions*.

WHAT MUST BE DISCUSSED

In holding discussions, the contracting officer must discuss the following with each offeror still being considered for award:

- **Deficiencies.** A deficiency is defined in FAR 15.001 as a material failure of a proposal to meet a government requirement, or a combination of significant weaknesses in a proposal that increases the risk of unsuccessful contract performance to an unacceptable level.
- **Significant weaknesses.** FAR 15.001 defines a significant weakness as a flaw in a proposal that appreciably increases the risk of unsuccessful performance.
- **Adverse past performance information.** This requirement is limited to information to which the offeror has not had an opportunity to respond.

The "still being considered for award" caveat is significant because FAR 15.306(d)(5) goes on to say that offerors may be eliminated from the competitive range whether or not material aspects of the proposal have been discussed or the offeror has been given an opportunity to submit a proposal revision. This means that, if it becomes clear during discussions that a proposal is no longer considered to be among the most highly rated and thus has no real opportunity to receive a contract award, the proposal may be eliminated from the competitive range even if the full range of meaningful discussions has not occurred.

In addition to the discussion of deficiencies, significant weaknesses, and certain adverse past performance information, FAR15.306(d)(3) encourages the contracting officer to discuss "other aspects" of the proposal that could, in the opinion of the contracting officer, be altered or explained to materially enhance the proposal's potential for award. These other aspects presumably include weaknesses. FAR 15.001 defines a *weakness* as a flaw in a proposal that increases the risk of unsuccessful contract performance.

DISCUSSING COST OR PRICE

Although the FAR does not address pricing or cost issues in any depth in its coverage of minimum requirements for discussions, it seems clear that any price or cost issue that would make a contractor proposal unacceptable could be classified as a deficiency. We also know that when the government did not inform a contractor that its price was too high or too low, the comptroller general has found in some instances in the past that meaningful discussions were not held. In one such opinion, the comptroller general opined that "discussions cannot be meaningful if the offeror is not apprised that its cost exceeds what the agency believes to be reasonable."

FAR 15.306 coverage on discussions does tell us at that the government "may suggest" to offerors, when appropriate, that their proposals might be more competitive if excesses were removed and the offered price decreased.

THE NEED FOR MEANINGFUL DISCUSSIONS

It would not be an overstatement to suggest that the component of government source selection that is most vulnerable to successful protest is the failure of the government to hold meaningful discussions. This may sometimes stem from government employees being so intent on following regulations and procedures on matters such as agency-required forms and prescribed communication chains that they lose sight of what they are trying to accomplish.

The object of holding discussions is to allow a competing contractor in the competitive range to revise its proposal and make it more attractive to the government, thus giving the competing contractor a reasonable opportunity for receiving an award. If the matters that would keep a competing contractor from being a legitimate contender for an award are not discussed, then discussions with that contractor are likely to be a meaningless charade and a waste of everyone's time and money. When only charade discussions can be held, the better course for both parties would have been to exclude the contractor from the competitive range.

To better understand meaningful discussions, it might be helpful to look at the generally accepted definitions for *deficiency* and *weakness* that existed before the current FAR definitions:

- **Deficiency:** Anything in a proposal that would make it unacceptable. This would include matters such as a too-risky technical approach, failure to meet a minimum government requirement as specified in the solicitation, failure to furnish all significant information required in the solicitation, and other such issues.
- **Weakness:** Anything in a proposal that is not a deficiency but that causes one contractor to be rated lower than another.

If an agency is going to hold discussions with a competing contractor with the goal of giving the contractor an opportunity to improve its proposal, then those discussions should cover all deficiencies and enough weaknesses that a suitably improved proposal could legitimately be a contender for the award. This could include giving the competing contractor an opportunity to respond to adverse past performance reports where applicable, identifying opportunities for technical improvements, and pointing out any excesses that may have unnecessarily increased the proposed cost or price.

Although a sufficient number (a judgment call by the contracting officer) of weaknesses should be discussed, including significant weaknesses (a mandatory requirement), it is not necessary to discuss all of them. The comptroller general has consistently held that the government is not required to spoon-feed a contractor during discussions.

In addition to the above elements, it should go without saying that the government must discuss any cost issues that would otherwise preclude a competing contractor from getting the award—for example, a cost that the government considers unreasonable.

THE MANNER AND SPECIFICITY OF DISCUSSIONS

The FAR does not dictate how discussions are to be held; and this matter is left to the discretion of the contracting officer. Discussions may be face-to-face, through letters or email, by telephone or videoconference, or any combination of these methods. When determining how discussions will be held, the contracting officer takes into consideration time and expense constraints, the complexity and magnitude of the issues to be discussed, and the need to maintain a clear and complete record of the discussions.

FAR 15.306 (d) requires that discussions be tailored to each offeror's proposal. Consequently, it is possible that the contracting officer could determine that only one or two issues will be discussed with one offeror, while a larger number of issues will be discussed with another. It is also possible that only one round of discussions will be held with one offeror but multiple rounds with another, as long as this disparity is not created to favor one offeror over another.

The contracting officer also gets to determine the specificity of discussions. For example, he or she may indicate that the government is concerned about the risk of the proposed technical approach. Or the contracting officer may not only tell the contractor that the government is concerned about the risk of the proposed technical approach, but also explain specifically *why* the government is concerned.

CONTRACTOR ALTERNATIVES IN DISCUSSIONS

When, during discussions, the contracting officer identifies deficiencies, weaknesses, or issues relating to cost, the competing contractor has three choices. It can revise the proposal, it can convince the contracting officer that the government's observations are incorrect, or it can do nothing. Those choices are business decisions that the competing contractor must make. By pointing these matters out, the government has met its obligations under the law.

Manager Alert

Like so many other elements of the source selection process, discussions require both compliance with law and regulation and the exercise of good business judgment. If acquisition officials wish to avoid protests centered on a failure to hold meaningful discussions, then they will make certain that all deficiencies, all pertinent cost/price issues, and enough weaknesses are discussed so that each contractor in the competitive range has an opportunity to improve its proposal to a point at which it could be a legitimate contender for contract award. While it is possible to get away with charade discussions—discussions that do not address the elements a competing contractor must improve in order to be a real contender for award—this may be too big a risk to take.

Chapter 29

PROHIBITED EXCHANGES

In the past, protest opinions and acquisition regulations addressed three practices that were prohibited when holding discussions: technical leveling, technical transfusion, and auctioning. Generally, these were defined as follows:

Technical leveling: Successive rounds of discussions on the same issues with the intent to bring an inferior proposal up to the level of others.

Technical transfusion: Introducing one competing contractor's ideas into another contractor's proposal. The government often did this by formulating leading questions during the discussion phase to coach a contractor to come up with the desired responses. Allegedly, it sometimes also occurred more overtly—for example, when one offeror's good ideas somehow found their way into the proposal of a favored contractor.

Another alleged aim of technical transfusion was to technically level competing contractors so that what the government really wanted from a technical proposal could be obtained from the competing contractor offering the lowest price.

Auctioning: The most common form of auctioning was setting one contractor against another to get a lower price without discussing any substantive price/cost issues. For example, Contractor A and Contractor B would be competing for a contract. A would be told that its price was higher than other offerors'. A would drop its price below that of contractor B. B would be told that its price was higher than competing prices, and so on.

Technical leveling, technical transfusion, and auctioning are not among the practices now prohibited in the FAR. However, they are terms that government acquisition professionals still commonly use.

FAR 15.306(e) now lists the following prohibited practices:

> Government personnel involved in the acquisition shall not engage in conduct that—
>
> (1) Favors one offeror over another;

(2) Reveals an offeror's technical solution, including unique technology, innovative and unique uses of commercial items, or any information that would compromise an offeror's intellectual property to another offeror;

(3) Reveals an offeror's price without that offeror's permission. However, the contracting officer may inform an offeror that its price is considered by the Government to be too high, or too low, and reveal the results of the analysis supporting that conclusion. It is also permissible, at the Government's discretion, to indicate to all offerors the cost or price that the Government's price analysis, market research, and other reviews have identified as reasonable;

(4) Reveals the names of individuals providing reference information about an offeror's past performance; or

(5) Knowingly furnishes source selection information in violation of [FAR] 3.104 and 41 U.S.C. 423(h)(1)(2)41.

FAVORING

Favoring one offeror over another has no well-defined limits, but most likely includes technical leveling and the "unfair competitive advantage" discussed in the coverage on presolicitation exchanges in Chapter 8. Like pornography, favoring cannot always be readily defined, but one should be able to recognize it when one sees it.

PROTECTION OF PROPRIETARY INFORMATION

The second limit on exchanges in FAR 15.306(e) replaces the prohibition on technical transfusion, but with greater clarity and an expanded scope.

LIMITS ON COST AND PRICE EXCHANGES

The third limit on exchanges requires some in-depth analysis. This addition to the FAR helps clarify that the type of hard bargaining on price that takes place in the private sector can also take place in government acquisition.

First, it provides that the government cannot reveal an offeror's price without that offeror's permission. (One situation in which the government requests offerors' permission to reveal price is in reverse auctioning, a price-oriented procurement method that does not ordinarily constitute a source selection as defined by the FAR.)

Next, it provides that the contracting officer may inform an offeror that its price is too high or too low and that the contracting officer may reveal the results of the analysis supporting that conclusion. The FAR does not limit the type of analysis that may be used. Thus, it appears that the government can tell a contractor that in comparison to other prices offered, or in comparison to the government estimate, its proposed price is too high.

The last price-/cost-oriented limitation provides that it is permissible, at the government's discretion, to indicate to all offerors the cost or price that the government's price analysis, market research, and other reviews have identified as reasonable. This seems to give the government the right to disclose the independent government cost estimate to contractors and to use it as a bargaining tool.

LIMITS ON THE RELEASE OF PAST PERFORMANCE INFORMATION

The fourth limit on exchanges prohibits the government from releasing the names of individuals providing reference information about an offeror's past performance. This limitation can also be found elsewhere in the FAR—for example, in the FAR coverage on debriefings.

PROTECTION OF SOURCE SELECTION INFORMATION

The final limitation on exchanges concerns the protection of source selection information. FAR Part 2 defines source selection information as the following information, provided that it has not previously been disclosed publicly:
- Bid prices
- Proposed costs or prices submitted in response to an agency solicitation
- Source selection plans
- Technical evaluation plans
- Technical evaluations of proposals
- Cost or price evaluations of proposals
- Competitive range determinations
- Rankings of bids, proposals, or competitors
- Reports and evaluations of source selection panels, boards, or advisory councils
- Other information marked as "source selection information" and as determined by the head of the agency or the contracting officer.

> **Manager Alert**
> Failure to comply with the limitations on exchanges, including protecting proprietary information, can result in sustained protests and/or other significant legal action against the government.

Chapter 30

PROPOSAL REVISIONS

FAR 15.307 requires the following with respect to allowing or requiring competing contractors to submit proposal revisions:

- If an offeror is eliminated before or after the competitive range is established, it will not be permitted to make further revisions to its proposal.
- When discussions are held with those in the competitive range, the contracting officer may request or allow interim proposal revisions to clarify and document understandings reached during discussions.
- At the conclusion of discussions, each offeror still in the competitive range is given an opportunity to submit a final proposal revision.
- The contracting officer is not required to establish a common cutoff date for any revisions that are permitted or required prior to the final proposal revision, but he or she must establish a common cutoff date for receipt of final proposal revisions.
- Requests for final proposal revisions shall advise offerors that the final proposal revisions must be in writing and that the government intends to make award without obtaining further revisions.

INTERIM REVISIONS

Interim proposal revisions may be in order when the issues being addressed during discussions are numerous or complex and the contracting officer wants to make sure the parties have a common understanding of what has been addressed, and perhaps agreed upon, prior to contractor submission of the final proposal revision.

REOPENING DISCUSSIONS

If after receiving final proposal revisions, it becomes clear to the contracting officer that some issues that must be resolved still remain, he or she can reopen discussions and give each offeror still in the competitive range an opportunity for another final proposal revision. This should be done only after careful consideration, however, for reasons that will become clear in the following section.

THE BAFO AND THE BARFO

In response to complaints by contractors that they were not being told when discussions were over, the government long ago adopted a procedure in which all contractors in the competitive range were notified that discussions were to be concluded by a certain time and date. The contractors were asked to submit their best and final offer by that time. The best and final offer was popularly called the *BAFO*.

Over time, the government began to misuse the BAFO procedure. In too many cases after the government had received final offers, some advisory person or group (or perhaps a source selection authority) would suggest that the contracting officer ought to be able to get a lower price. So competing contractors were told they were being given an opportunity to submit another BAFO. Often these "opportunity letters" did not address any discussion issues at all, but contractors sensed they were being asked to sharpen their pencils and to come up with a more attractive price. Sometimes these new BAFO "opportunities" were given to competing contractors multiple times on the same source selection. Contractors bitterly began to distinguish between the BAFO (best and final offer) and the BARFO (best and *really* final offer).

Contractors complained to government officials about the BAFO, and some government officials vowed to abolish it. However, when they set about to abolish the BAFO, it was obvious that a common cutoff date was still necessary. So the request for a BAFO by a common cutoff date became a request for a final proposal revision by a common cutoff date. Except for the language used, the procedures seem remarkably the same—and so does the potential for abuse. Asking for multiple "final" revisions without a compelling reason to do so would seem to be as questionable a practice as asking for multiple BAFOs.

> **Manager Alert**
> Although the term *best and final offer* no longer appears in the FAR, many contractor personnel and government officials, in conversational situations, still call the final proposal revision the BAFO.

EVALUATION AFTER FINAL PROPOSAL REVISIONS

Once final proposal revisions are received, the government conducts evaluations to take into account any changes and additional information furnished by the competing contractors, and the evaluators submit a new summary report to the contracting officer and source selection authority. Depending on the regulations or practices of the agency and/or the wishes of the source selection authority, the final summary report may or may not contain a recommendation for award. Some source selection authorities prefer to have a recommendation to consider. Others prefer that there not be a recommendation so that if the source selection authority does not agree with the recommendation, there is no paper trail showing disagreement. Regardless, the source selection authority has autonomy in selecting the source, and there is nothing improper in making an independent decision that would not have been the decision made by others, including evaluators and advisors.

Chapter 31

MAKING AND DOCUMENTING THE SOURCE SELECTION DECISION

The FAR makes it crystal clear that the source selection authority has autonomy in making the source selection decision (15.308):

> The source selection authority's (SSA) decision shall be based on a comparative assessment of proposals against all source selection criteria in the solicitation. While the SSA may use reports and analyses prepared by others, the source selection decision shall represent the SSA's independent judgment. The source selection decision shall be documented, and the documentation shall include the rationale for any business judgments and tradeoffs made or relied on by the SSA, including benefits associated with additional costs. Although the rationale for the selection decision must be documented, that documentation need not quantify the tradeoffs that led to the decision.

On occasion, SSAs have asked for reevaluations, have performed reevaluations themselves, or have otherwise gone against the advice of evaluators. And these are, in specific circumstances, perfectly acceptable things to do when the source selection authority has a reasonable basis for doing them. Case law makes clear that the SSA, when making the source selection decision, is normally held to only two standards:

1. The decision must be reasonable (sometimes the comptroller general says *rational*)
2. The decision must be consistent with the promises the government made or implied in the solicitation.

A PERSUASIVE SALES DOCUMENT

FAR 15.308 also tells us that the source selection must be documented and that the documentation shall include the reasoning behind business judgments made, including any benefits associated with additional costs. In a lowest price, technically acceptable source selection, this is relatively easy to do since award is made to the lowest price among acceptable proposals. But for trade-off selections, the documentation requires greater thought and greater clarity.

The source selection document should be looked upon as a sales document designed to convince others that a rational decision was made. It should be accurate, complete, and persuasive. It may turn out to be the only significant defense the government has in the event of a protest against the source selection decision.

QUANTIFYING THE DECISION

Although the rationale for selection must be documented, it is not necessary to quantify the trade-offs that led to the decision. Agencies that historically have quantified trade-off decisions usually did so in one of two ways:

1. By "scoring" costs (as discussed in Chapter 13). The contractor with the highest combined total of non-cost points and cost points normally received the contract award.
2. Explaining specific estimated cost impacts in a narrative fashion. For example, a source selection document might say:

    > Contractor A has far more favorable past performance ratings and more experience in the maintenance and repair of test equipment and has been rated higher than other competing contractors by the technical evaluation team. By selecting contractor A, it can be expected that the agency would experience at least 20 percent less equipment downtime and avoid the consequent expensive testing delays, especially in the early months of the contract. Since schedule delay can cost the agency as much as $50,000 per day, the adverse cost impact of choosing any of the other competitors could possibly exceed $750,000. The proposed cost of contractor A's proposal is only $250,000 more than any other competitor's. Thus, it is clear that award to contractor A will yield the best value.

Some cynical observers have characterized this type of approach as an attempt to draw a mathematically precise line from an unwarranted assumption to a foregone conclusion. Nonetheless, it is an acceptable method of quantification if the assumptions made and conclusions reached are reasonable and defensible.

DOCUMENTING THE DECISION WITHOUT QUANTIFICATION

All that would really be necessary to justify the selection of contractor A in our abbreviated and simplified example would be a statement without any specific quantification:

> The proposal of contractor A was the highest-rated proposal and received a rating of "outstanding" on all evaluation factors. It was particularly strong in the areas of past performance and relevant experience. Taking advantage of these strengths will most assuredly result in significant reduction in equipment downtime and reduction of delays in critical and expensive testing. These advantages more than offset any differences in proposed cost when compared to other proposals considered.

Of course, the source selection authority could have opted for a lower-priced proposal even if non-cost factors were significantly more important than costs. And, as might be noted, the source selection authority in our example did not address all of the evaluation factors, only those that were significant in making the selection. A comptroller general opinion addressed both issues when it said:

> Notwithstanding a solicitation's emphasis on technical merit, an agency may properly select a lower-priced, lower technically rated proposal if it decides that the cost premium involved in selecting a higher rated, higher priced proposal is not justified given the acceptable level of technical competence available at the lower price.

> An agency need not address each and every feature of a proposal in documenting a source selection decision, but must show only that its evaluation conclusions are reasonably based (ViroMed Laboratories, Inc., B-310747.4, January 22, 2009).

SOURCE SELECTION RECORDS

FAR15.305 requires that source selection records include an evaluation of each offeror's ability to accomplish the technical requirements—specifically, a summary, matrix, or quantitative ranking, along with an appropriate supporting narrative assessment of each technical proposal, based on the evaluation factors. Usually, the summary reports of evaluators, advisors, or both fulfill this requirement. However, the SSA is not bound by such reports, and the FAR requirement can be met through documents independently prepared by the SSA.

ADVICE FROM EVALUATORS AND SUPERIORS

A number of agencies may require the SSA, either as normal practice or on a case-by-case basis, to brief a superior before announcing a source selection decision.

And, in almost all cases, the SSA receives advice from evaluators and advisors. The SSA's freedom to deviate from evaluators' and superiors' recommendations was addressed in National Steel and Shipbuilding Company, B-281142.2, January 4, 1999, when the comptroller general found that:

> Any decision of the source selection authority must be independent, and if it is shown that the decision was coerced, it is likely that the decision can be overturned. Some agencies have a practice of a source selection authority announcing a decision only after he or she first briefs and presumably gets advice from a superior. They should tread lightly here to avoid any actual or perceived impediment to the independence of the source selection authority. Under a best value evaluation scheme, evaluation ratings and scores are only guides to assist source selection officials in evaluating proposals. PRC, Inc., B-274698.2, B-274698.3, Jan. 23, 1997, 97-1 CPD para. 115 at 12. Source selection officials, which includes officials at an intermediate level, are not bound by the recommendations or evaluation judgments of lower-level evaluators, even though the evaluators normally may be expected to have the technical experience required for such evaluations.

TRADING COST FOR QUALITY

The significant flexibility and discretion afforded the source selection authority in making cost/merit trade-offs was again demonstrated in DynCorp et al., B-257037.2, December 15, 1994, where the comptroller general addressed the protest of a contract award made under a solicitation for base operations and support in the Middle East. In that case, the source selection authority selected a contractor that had received an evaluation score of 82.48 points, as opposed to a contractor that had received an evaluation score of 80.37 points, even though the probable cost of the selected contractor was $22 million more than the cost of the contractor that had received 80.37 points. Source selection documentation indicated that the primary advantage of the winning contractor was a more realistic staffing level.

The unsuccessful contractors joined together to protest the award. Among other issues, the protestors maintained that it was unreasonable for the Army to conclude that the small numerical technical superiority (about 2 points out of 100) was worth up to $22 million in additional costs, especially since the evaluation scheme in the RFP granted only slightly more importance to technical quality. In his opinion, the comptroller general stated:

> Agencies may make cost/technical tradeoffs in deciding between competing proposals; the propriety of such a tradeoff turns not on the difference in technical scores or ratings *per se*, but on whether the selection official's judgment concerning the significance of that difference was reasonable and adequately justified in light of the RFP evaluation scheme. . . . [W]e cannot

conclude that the Army acted unreasonably in determining that ITT's . . . proposal . . . represented the best value to the government.

THE SUBJECTIVE NATURE OF DECISIONS

The source selection decision for trade-off procurements is much like many other elements of that process. It tends to be subjective, and, in many cases, different officials could come to different conclusions.

> **Manager Alert**
> Despite the challenging number of regulations and policies that acquisition officials must follow throughout the source selection process, sound business judgment remains essential to a competent and successful source selection. That sound judgment must be demonstrated throughout the process, culminating in the selection of the source and the persuasive and complete documentation of the source selection decision.

Chapter 32

NOTIFICATIONS TO OFFERORS

FAR Part 15 provides for both preaward and postaward notices to unsuccessful contractors.

PREAWARD NOTIFICATION

The FAR requires two types of preaward notices:
- FAR 15.503(a)(1) requires that "the contracting officer shall promptly notify offerors in writing when their proposals are excluded from the competitive range or otherwise eliminated from competition. The notification shall state the basis for the determination and that a proposal revision will not be considered."
- FAR 15.503(a)(2) requires a preaward notice at completion of negotiations (discussions) and completion of determinations of responsibility—*but before award*—whenever there is:
    o A small business set-aside
    o A benefit given to a small disadvantaged business concern
    o Use of HUBzone procedures
    o Use of service-disabled veteran-owned small business procedures.

The latter type of preaward notice identifies the source tentatively selected. It gives other offerors an opportunity to challenge the claimed socioeconomic status of that source before award is actually made. Such notice need not be made if a procurement has been set aside under the 8(a) program for small disadvantaged (minority) businesses or when the contracting officer has determined that award must be made without delay.

In addition to giving competitors the right to challenge the claimed status of the apparently successful contractor, this preaward notice also allows unsuccessful offerors to seek out subcontracting opportunities before the contract award is publicly announced.

POSTAWARD NOTIFICATION

Pursuant to FAR 15.503(b), the contracting officer must, within three days after award, provide a written postaward notice to each offeror whose proposal was in the competitive range but was not selected for award. This notice shall include

- The number of offerors solicited
- The number of proposals received
- The name and address of each offeror receiving an award
- Items, quantity, and price information
- In general terms, the reasons why the offeror's proposal was not accepted (unless the price information reveals the reason, as may be the case in an lowest price, technically acceptable selection).

FAR 15.504 requires that the successful contractor be notified "by furnishing the executed contract or other notice of award."

Chapter 33

DEBRIEFINGS

Many of the government rules for source selection are there to protect the interests of the seller and go beyond protections that would normally be found in private sector buyer-seller relationships. One of these special perks is the furnishing of a detailed debriefing by the buyer. Debriefings may be given to a competing contractor before or after a source selection is made, but a competing contractor is not entitled to both.

PREAWARD DEBRIEFINGS

FAR 15.505 includes these provisions for preaward debriefings:
- They may be requested by offerors within three days after receiving notice that they have been excluded from the competitive range or otherwise eliminated from the competition.
- The contracting officer must furnish the debriefing as soon as practicable but can delay the debriefing until after award if such delay is determined to be in the best interest of the government.
- Preaward debriefings are limited to discussion of the offeror's proposal (e.g., deficiencies and weaknesses) and issues involving the source selection process.
- The excluded offeror may instead elect to have a postaward debriefing, at which it could obtain more information than it would be given in a preaward debriefing; however, this could negatively affect an offeror's ability to submit a timely protest should it wish to protest after the debriefing.

If an offeror elects to have a preaward debriefing, there will be no discussion at all about the content or rating of other proposals or any discussion of relative standing. The FAR prohibits the disclosure of:
- The number of offerors
- The identity of other offerors

- The content of other offerors' proposals
- The ranking of other offerors
- The evaluation of other offerors
- The release of any information that would be prohibited in a postaward debriefing.

POSTAWARD DEBRIEFINGS

FAR 15.506 sets forth the following provisions for postaward debriefings:

> The competing contractors that were not eligible for a preaward debriefing must request a postaward debriefing within three days after receiving notice that an award has been made. Requests submitted after this time do not have to be honored, but the contracting officer has the discretion to honor them if he or she wishes.
>
> The contracting officer should arrange for the debriefing within five days after receipt of a request. If this is not practicable, the debriefing should be given as soon as circumstances permit. (Note that if a contractor learns of a protestable issue at a debriefing, the timely-protest clock starts ticking at that moment. It is usually to the advantage of the government to schedule debriefings as quickly as possible to minimize the cost impact of any delay occasioned by a subsequent protest.)

Offerors are given much more information in a postaward debriefing than they would have received in a preaward debriefing. Information to be furnished by the government includes:

- Significant weaknesses and deficiencies in the offeror's proposal.
- The overall evaluated price and technical rating of both the successful contractor and the contractor being debriefed. (Point-by-point comparisons are not permitted.)
- Past performance information on the debriefed offeror. This may not include the names of individuals providing information about the offeror's past performance.
- The ranking of offers, if a ranking was developed. Most agencies just select the successful contractor(s) and do not rank offers.
- A summary of the rationale for award.
- For commercial items, the make and model of the item to be delivered by the successful offeror.

RESPONSES TO RELEVANT QUESTIONS

FAR 15.505 (e) (3) provides, in both preaward and postaward debriefings, that debriefed offerors are also entitled to "reasonable responses to relevant questions about whether source selection procedures contained in the solicitation, applicable regulations, and other applicable authorities were followed." This allows offerors to further explore government actions taken during the source selection process to determine whether they believe the contracting officer and the source selection authority followed the rules regarding matters such as consistency with solicitation promises and the conduct of meaningful discussions.

INFORMATION THAT MAY NOT BE FURNISHED

Information that may not be made available in either preaward or postaward debriefings includes:

- Point-by-point comparisons between the debriefed offeror's proposal and those of other offerors.
- Competing contractors' proposals.
- Information not available under the Freedom of Information Act.
- Trade secrets.
- Privileged or confidential manufacturing processes and techniques.
- Commercial and financial information that is privileged or confidential. This includes cost breakdowns, profit, indirect cost rates, and other similar information.
- The names of individuals providing reference information about an offeror's past performance.

Both preaward and postaward debriefings must be summarized in official documents, which are made a part of the contract file.

Manager Alert

Ostensibly, debriefings are given to help competing contractors do better in future acquisitions, and they can be very valuable in this regard. However, there is no question that contractors often come to debriefings in a less-than-conciliatory frame of mind. They have invested blood, sweat, tears, and money in a proposal. Sometimes, losing a contract can have a profoundly adverse impact on a company and those who work for that company. If an offeror is not convinced at the debriefing that it was treated fairly and in accordance with the rules, a protest may follow.

THE MANNER OF DEBRIEFINGS

Contracting officers get to determine how a debriefing will be given (for example, by mail, by telephone, or face-to-face). In selections that involve a substantial amount of money or are otherwise of significant sensitivity or import, many contracting officers opt for a face-to-face debriefing, where they can interact more personally with contractor personnel.

PREPARING FOR FACE-TO-FACE DEBRIEFINGS

When preparing for and conducting a face-to-face debriefing, contracting officers should:

- Ask for the contractor's questions in advance so that the government can be better prepared to answer them.
- Ask key personnel, who may include evaluators, program officials, contract specialists, and legal counsel, to help them prepare for and present the debriefing.
- Prepare for any additional questions that might arise during the debriefing.
- Prepare an agenda beforehand to keep the meeting on track and to address matters in a logical sequence.
- Impress on team members the sensitivity involved and the need to treat the contractor with courtesy and respect.

It is important that the contracting officer control the government's share of dialogue during a debriefing to avoid any slips of the tongue that might precipitate a protest—for example, erroneously characterizing a weakness as a deficiency, or pointing out flaws that evaluators perceived in a proposal when those flaws had no bearing on evaluation ratings or the source selection decision. Although such slips may not result in a sustained protest, they can lead to protests, with their accompanying delay, cost, and ill will.

LESSONS LEARNED

In summary, competing contractors are entitled to a debriefing. It is their right under the law. Debriefings can be valuable as lessons learned for those competing contractors that were not successful in obtaining a contract. Properly conducted, debriefings can also offer reassurance to those contractors that they were treated fairly and in accordance with law and regulation.

THE END OF THE PROCESS

Unless an offeror files a protest, postaward debriefings mark the completion of the source selection process.

Chapter 34

TASK ORDER CONTRACTS

When the Federal Acquisition Streamlining Act (FASA) was passed in 1994, it provided for the first time that indefinite delivery contracts could be awarded for services. These indefinite delivery contracts for services are called *task order contracts*, and they led to a huge transformation in the way much of government contracting was conducted.

Before FASA, an agency that needed an environmental study, for example, would go through the entire source selection process, which often took 180 days or more. The agency would have to do the same thing again when it needed to remove contaminated soil, or restore a damaged ecosystem, or study the flow of contaminants in an aquifer.

With the passage of FASA, an indefinite delivery contract could be awarded for environmental remediation services, with individual task orders being issued under the contract as specific environmental remediation needs arose. Thus, the procurement administrative lead time for each individual requirement could be reduced to a small fraction of what it was before.

The vast majority of these contracts for services were characterized as being indefinite quantity contracts, since the government was not able to predict in advance the number and specific character of the tasks that would ultimately be awarded under the contract.

THE SOURCE SELECTION PROCESS FOR TASK ORDER CONTRACTS

The processes for selecting contractors for indefinite delivery/indefinite quantity (ID/IQ) contracts are essentially the same as the processes we have discussed throughout this book, with two significant exceptions:
1. The preference for award of multiple contracts
2. The use of sample task orders.

PREFERENCE FOR MULTIPLE AWARDS

FAR Part 16 establishes a preference for multiple awards of ID/IQ contracts (except for contracts for certain advisory and assistance services and some other limited exceptions) so that there can be competition for task orders among contract holders whenever appropriate. The FAR does not address how many contracts should be awarded but leaves this matter up to agency acquisition officials. Among the factors to be considered are:
- The scope and complexity of the requirement
- The expected duration and frequency of task orders
- The mix of resources a contractor must have to perform task requirements
- The ability to maintain competition among awardees.

THE USE OF SAMPLE TASKS

Since the government may not have at hand a specific task that encompasses the general range of services that will be needed under an ID/IQ contract, or may not have any immediate tasks at all, it is common practice for agencies to require competing contractors to base their technical and cost proposals in part on government-prepared sample tasks that encompass a reasonable range of the expected services. Competing contractors are then evaluated on how they would propose to go about performing the sample tasks.

The use of sample tasks has been the topic of some academic discussion among acquisition professionals. It was felt by some of these professionals that requiring competing contractors to submit proposals for make-believe work could result in overly optimistic proposals, since competing contractors would not have to live up to the promises they made. Because of this, agencies strive, whenever possible, to have competing contractors submit proposals on actual tasks that can be awarded at the time the basic contracts are awarded. This helps to ensure that task proposals are more realistic, especially regarding costs.

PROVIDING FOR THE AWARD OF TASK ORDERS

The ID/IQ contracts that are awarded must describe the procedures the government will use to issue individual task orders and must identify a minimum and a maximum amount of services that the government will order. The example solicitation provisions shown in Appendix I are for a proposed task order contract.

AWARDING INDIVIDUAL TASK ORDERS

FAR Part 16 contains the guidance used when selecting a task order contract holder for a particular task. Substantially this guidance is as follows:

- With very limited exceptions, the contracting officer must provide each contract holder a "fair opportunity to be considered" (FAR 16.505(b)(1)) for each order exceeding $3,000.
- The contracting officer has broad discretion in developing order-placement procedures and should keep contractor submission requirements to a minimum.
- Streamlining procedures, including oral presentations, can be used.
- If the contracting officer has information available to ensure each of the multiple awardees was provided a fair opportunity to be considered, then it is not necessary to contact each task order contractor if the order does not exceed $5 million. If the order does exceed $5 million, each awardee must be notified of the requirement and the significant factors and subfactors (and their relative importance) to be used in selecting a contract holder for the task. Furthermore, after the task order is awarded, each unsuccessful awardee is entitled to receive a notification of the task order award and may receive a debriefing.

    Order-placement procedures for actual task orders must be consistent with the placement guidance provided to contractors in the initial contract. Accordingly, this order placement guidance should be carefully tailored.
- Documentation of the basis for award is required.

THE ROLE OF THE OMBUDSMAN

The head of each agency must appoint an ombudsman to review complaints from contractors and ensure that they are given a fair opportunity to be considered. The ombudsman must be a senior agency official who is independent of the contracting officer.

> **Manager Alert**
> The manner in which a contractor is given a "fair opportunity to be considered" may vary widely from contract to contract and from agency to agency. In one case, the contracting officer may, for example, examine all basic contract awardees and determine that only one or two have the wherewithal to perform a given task. The excluded contractors were given a "fair opportunity" in that their qualifications, past performance, experience, and perhaps current workload were considered by the contracting officer. In another situation, the contracting officer could determine that all basic contract awardees should be given an opportunity to compete for the task. The contracting officer normally relies a great deal on technical advice, such as that provided by the project office, in making these decisions.

POTENTIAL FOR STREAMLINING

Task order contracts offer opportunities for streamlining the competitive award of individual tasks. Returning to our environmental services contract example, assume that four contracts have been awarded and that the government has already gathered information on each contractor's past performance, corporate experience, and personnel, among other factors. To award a task for an environmental study, the government might ask the four contractors for only the following:

- A signed price offer
- An oral presentation on how each plans to accomplish the task.

On the strength of this information, the government could select a contractor for award of the task. A process that once took months can be completed in a few weeks.

Chapter 35

VARIATIONS IN SOURCE SELECTION

There are a number of alternatives to conventional source selection. Knowledge of these variations could prove valuable to the government manager.

THE ADVISORY MULTISTEP SELECTION PROCESS

The advisory multistep process described at FAR 15.202 allows agencies to publish a presolicitation notice at the governmentwide point of entry, FedBizOpps. This notice describes the planned acquisition and invites potential offerors to submit specific information that the government feels it needs in order to assess their potential to be viable competitors. The government then advises each of the responding potential offerors whether it is deemed to be a viable competitor.

If an offeror is subsequently advised that it is not considered to be a viable competitor, the government must inform the offeror of the general basis for that opinion. The offeror must also be notified that, notwithstanding the advice furnished by the government, it may still participate in the resultant source selection process if it wishes to do so.

A carefully crafted advisory presolicitation notice can save contractors with little chance of receiving award from going to the expense of developing a full-blown proposal. Such a notice also allows the government to save time and money since it will reduce instances where it is necessary to evaluate proposals that have no realistic probability of being awarded the contract.

ARCHITECT-ENGINEER SERVICES

The procedures for selecting a source for architect-engineer (AE) services are described in FAR Part 36. While AE acquisitions are considered to be competitive for the purposes of the Competition in Contracting Act, competing contractors for AE services do not normally compete on cost, only on non-cost factors.

These procedures are based on a law commonly referred to as the Brooks Act, which seeks to make sure that quality AE services are acquired at a fair and reasonable cost, instead of merely acceptable services being acquired at a lower cost.

FAR 36.602-1 requires that the following selection criteria be used for AE acquisitions:

- Professional qualifications
- Specialized experience and technical competence in the type of work required
- Capacity to perform on time
- Location in the general geographical area of and knowledge of the locality of the project (unless this would result in an inappropriate number of competitors)
- Conceptual design, when appropriate and when approved by the agency head or designee
- Other appropriate criteria.

The selection process can be summarized in eight steps:

1. An agency issues a public notice for a requirement, and an evaluation board reviews responses to this public notice and reviews current data files on eligible firms.
2. At least three firms are selected as the most highly qualified. These contractors constitute what is commonly called the *short list*.
3. The evaluation board prepares a detailed report for the source selection authority and recommends, in order of preference, at least three of the evaluated competitors.
4. The source selection authority may go along with the order of preference recommended or may establish one of his or her own.
5. The source selection team conducts negotiations with the most preferred contractor.
6. If agreement is reached, the agency awards a contract.
7. If agreement cannot be reached, then negotiations begin with the next firm on the preferred list.
8. If the preferred list is exhausted without agreement being reached, the selection authority may direct the evaluation board to recommend additional firms.

FAR 36.602-2(a) provides that members of the evaluation board "shall be appointed from among highly qualified professional employees of the agency or other agencies" and may include "private practitioners."

COMMERCIAL ITEM PROCUREMENT

The FAR's definition for a *commercial item* is extensive. It includes not only products sold to the general public, but many services as well. It even includes products evolving from items sold to the general public that have not yet been offered for sale.

The FAR requires that acquisitions of commercial items be made pursuant to FAR Part 12. The simplified source selection procedures found in FAR Part 13 or the more complex source selection procedures detailed in FAR Part 15 may be used in acquiring commercial items. However, in the event of any conflict in the FAR guidance, FAR Part 12 applies.

Although the source selection processes that we have discussed at length in this book will often apply to source selection for commercial item acquisitions, there are two major differences: the forms and formats to be used and the solicitation provisions required by the FAR.

Rather than using the uniform contract format (UCF) that is common in most requests for proposals, written solicitations for commercial items (other than combined solicitations/synopses, which are discussed below) use Standard Form (SF) 1449. This standard form may be used as a request for quotations, a request for proposals, or an invitation for bids. (Invitations for bids do not use non-cost evaluation factors, and the source selection procedures described in this book are not applicable to them.)

When using SF 1449, there are standard commercial item provisions in the FAR that substitute for Sections L and M of the UCF. When appropriate, the contracting officer may tailor these standard provisions. Tailored provisions are attached to SF 1449 and form a part of the solicitation.

Market research plays a big part in what will be required of offerors in the tailored provisions. For example, offerors should not be asked for unique technical proposals when market research indicates that available product literature provides enough information for the government to perform any needed evaluations.

Evaluation factors such as small business matters, past performance, quality, suitability, and price/cost can all be used as evaluation factors in selecting a contractor for a commercial item acquisition. However, while source selections for commercial item acquisitions can sometimes resemble the source selections described in this book, many—perhaps most—commercial item competitions are based on price alone.

STREAMLINED SOLICITATION FOR COMMERCIAL ITEMS

The FAR provides for a streamlined method of solicitation that combines the synopsis requirement at the governmentwide point of entry, FedBizOpps, with the solicitation itself. The SF 1499 is not used for a combined solicitation/synopsis. Instead, the notice of the procurement is expanded to include a request for an offer (quotation or proposal) and any evaluation factors and their relative importance, where applicable. Detailed procedures for this method appear in FAR Parts 5 and 12.

BROAD AGENCY ANNOUNCEMENTS

FAR 35.016 tells us that a broad agency announcement (BAA) is a competitive solicitation procedure used to obtain proposals for basic and applied research. It also is used "for that part of development [that is] not related to the development of a specific system or hardware procurement."

The BAA offers a great deal more flexibility to the scientific and technical community than is available under conventional source selection procedures. Some have characterized the BAA as a process that allows the government buyer to go window shopping in the marketplace of ideas. Some of the differences between a FAR Part 15 source selection for research and development using an RFP and one using a BAA are summarized in the following table:

Requests For Proposals	Broad Agency Announcement
Normally focuses on a specific system or hardware solution.	Focuses on scientific study and experimentation directed toward advancing the state of the art or increasing knowledge or understanding.
The government uses a requirements document setting forth a work statement or performance objectives against which all offerors must propose.	The government identifies a problem to be addressed or an area of general research interest. Each offeror then proposes its own statement of work and technical approach.
Winner is selected by comparing proposals.	Proposals contain stand-alone, unique solutions. They are not compared to one another.
Consideration of proposals follows a predetermined source selection plan.	Proposals undergo a scientific review process. A proposal that is otherwise weak could be selected if it shows great technical promise, such as a risky but perhaps revolutionary approach.

Common features of conventional source selections and BAA source selections generally include:
- Publicizing the requirement at the governmentwide point of entry (FedBizOpps)
- Identifying selection criteria in the solicitation
- Considering cost realism/reasonableness.

Chapter 36

ETHICAL CONSIDERATIONS IN SOURCE SELECTION

It is not unusual for the mass media to report on alleged or actual illegal activity involving federal government contracting. And I suppose we shouldn't be surprised. Willie Sutton, a career criminal, once said he robbed banks because "that's where the money is." And there is a great deal of money involved in government contracting.

PRINCIPLES FOR ALL GOVERNMENT EMPLOYEES

The Office of Government Ethics developed a list of principles that apply to the ethical conduct of all government employees, not just those involved in contracting. These principles were made applicable to all government employees by an executive order of the president. Because a number of these principles have a direct bearing on people involved in source selection, we have included the list here; see Exhibit 36-1.

THE PROCUREMENT INTEGRITY ACT

There is a law designed to address the source selection process in particular. In response to highly publicized situations where competing contractors were given inside information by government employees, and to situations in which it was perceived by Congress and the public that contractors were being treated favorably so that government officials could later gain employment with the contractors, Congress passed the Procurement Integrity Act in 1988 and last amended it in 1996. A Department of Justice outline of the provisions of the act is shown in Exhibit 36-2.

> **Manager Alert**
> Notwithstanding any efforts to legislate ethics, proper conduct in source selection always comes down to personal integrity. Some people just seem to be more disposed toward unethical behavior than others. Not infrequently, major fraud on government contracts is committed by people who are especially hardworking and capable.

AVOIDING THE APPEARANCE OF IMPROPRIETY

FAR 3.101-1 tells us, "While many Federal laws and regulations place restrictions on the actions of Government personnel, their official conduct must, in addition, be such that they would have no reluctance to make a full public disclosure of their actions."

Similarly, many people who conduct ethics training advocate following the *Washington Post* rule of thumb (sometimes called the *New York Times* rule of thumb) when performing day-to-day duties. This is essentially a prescription that officials make only those decisions or take those actions that they would not be reluctant to have reported the next day on the front page of the *Washington Post*.

EXHIBIT 36-1
Principles of Ethical Conduct for Government Officers and Employees

(a) Public service is a public trust, requiring employees to place loyalty to the Constitution, the laws, and ethical principles above private gain.

(b) Employees shall not hold financial interests that conflict with the conscientious performance of duty.

(c) Employees shall not engage in financial transactions using nonpublic Government information or allow the improper use of such information to further any private interest.

(d) An employee shall not, except pursuant to such reasonable exceptions as are provided by regulation, solicit or accept any gift or other item of monetary value from any person or entity seeking official action from, doing business with, or conducting activities regulated by the employee's agency, or whose interests may be substantially affected by the performance or nonperformance of the employee's duties.

(e) Employees shall put forth honest effort in the performance of their duties.

(f) Employees shall make no unauthorized commitments or promises of any kind purporting to bind the Government.

(g) Employees shall not use public office for private gain.

(h) Employees shall act impartially and not give preferential treatment to any private organization or individual.

(i) Employees shall protect and conserve Federal property and shall not use it for other than authorized activities.

(j) Employees shall not engage in outside employment or activities, including seeking or negotiating for employment, that conflict with official Government duties and responsibilities.

(k) Employees shall disclose waste, fraud, abuse, and corruption to appropriate authorities.

(l) Employees shall satisfy in good faith their obligations as citizens, including all just financial obligations, especially those—such as Federal, State, or local taxes—that are imposed by law.

(m) Employees shall adhere to all laws and regulations that provide equal opportunity for all Americans regardless of race, color, religion, sex, national origin, age, or handicap.

(n) Employees shall endeavor to avoid any actions creating the appearance that they are violating the law or the ethical standards promulgated pursuant to this order.

Source: Executive Order 12731, October 17, 1990.

EXHIBIT 36-2
Department of Justice Outline of the Procurement Integrity Act

I. Disclosing and Obtaining Contractor Bid or Proposal Information or Source Selection Information

   A. A present or former employee of, or person acting on behalf of or advising, the U.S. on a procurement, who has or had access to such information shall not disclose it before the award of the contract to which the information relates. (48 CFR 3.104-4(a))

   B. No person shall knowingly obtain such information before the award of the contract to which the information relates. (48 CFR 3.104-4(b))

II. Offers of Non-Federal Employment

   An official participating personally and substantially in a procurement for a contract in excess of the **simplified acquisition threshold** ($100,000) who is contacted by a bidder regarding non-federal employment during the conduct of the procurement shall:

   A. Report the contact to his supervisor and the [Designated Agency Ethics Official] DAEO in writing; and

   B. Reject the offer; or

   C. Disqualify himself in writing to the Head of the Contracting Activity in accordance with 18 U.S.C. § 208 until authorized to resume on grounds that:

      1. the offeror is no longer a bidder; or

      2. all discussions have terminated without an agreement for employment. (48 CFR 3.104-4(c))

   D. This requirement does not apply after the award of the contract or after the procurement has been canceled, although 18 U.S.C. § 208 would still require disqualification on the part of an employee who is administering a contract.

III. Accepting Compensation from a Contractor

   A. A former official may not accept compensation from a contractor within a year after he served as the procuring contracting officer, the source selection authority, a member of the source selection evaluation board or the chief of a financial or technical evaluation team for a procurement for a contract in excess of $10 million awarded to that contractor.

   B. The above restriction also applies to a former official who served as program manager, deputy program manager or administrative contracting officer for a contract over $10 million.

Chapter 36: Ethical Considerations in Source Selection

    C. It applies to a former official who made a decision to:
        1. award a contract, modification, subcontract, task order or delivery order, in excess of $10 million;
        2. establish overhead or other rates applicable to a contract in excess of $10 million; or
        3. approve issuance of a contract payment or payments in excess of $10 million, or pay or settle a claim in excess of $10 million. (48 CFR 3.104-4(d))
    D. Note that this restriction can apply to decisions made after the award of the contract which need not be competitively awarded. The restriction does not apply to accepting compensation from a division or affiliate of the contractor that does not produce the same or similar product or service.
    E. The one-year prohibition on accepting compensation begins:
        1. on the date of selection of the contractor for a former official who served in a position listed in paragraph A at that time, but not on the date of the award of the contract;
        2. on the date of the award of the contract for [an] official who served in a position listed in paragraph A at that time whether or not he was serving at the time of selection;
        3. on the last date an official served in a position listed in paragraph B; or
        4. on the date a decision listed in paragraph C was made.

IV. Definitions
    A. Contractor bid or proposal information means information not made available to the public and includes:
        1. cost or pricing data;
        2. indirect costs and direct labor rates;
        3. proprietary information about manufacturing processes, operations or techniques; and
        4. information marked by the contractor as "contractor bid or proposal information."
    B. Source selection information means information not made available to the public and includes:
        1. bid prices;
        2. proposed costs or prices from bidders;
        3. source selection and technical evaluation plans;

> 4. technical evaluations, cost or price evaluations, competitive range determinations, rankings of bids, reports of source selection panels; and
> 5. other information marked as "source selection" based on a determination that its disclosure would jeopardize the procurement.
>
> Source: U.S. Department of Justice Procurement Integrity page. Available at www.justice.gov/jmd/ethics/procure.html. Accessed October 2012.

ACRONYMS AND ABBREVIATIONS

ADR	alternative dispute resolution
AE	architect-engineer
AP	acquisition plan
BAA	broad agency announcement
BAFO	best and final offer
BARFO	best and really final offer
CICA	Competition in Contracting Act
COC	certificate of competency
DCMA	Defense Contract Management Agency
DoD	Department of Defense/Defense Department
EPLS	Excluded Parties List System
FAPIIS	Federal Awardee Performance and Integrity Information System
FAR	Federal Acquisition Regulation
FASA	Federal Acquisition Streamlining Act
FedBizOpps	Federal Business Opportunities
GAO	Government Accountability Office
GPE	governmentwide point of entry
GSA	General Services Administration
HUBZone	historically underutilized business zone
ID/IQ	indefinite delivery/indefinite quantity [contract]
IFB	invitation for bids
IFN	item for negotiation [form]
IGCE	independent government cost estimate
IPT	integrated product team
LPTA	lowest price, technically acceptable
NAICS	North American Industry Classification System
NDI	nondevelopmental item(s)
OGE	Office of Government Ethics
OMB	Office of Management and Budget

PALT	procurement administrative lead time
PCO	procuring/principal contracting officer
PEB	proposal evaluation board
PPIRS	Past Performance Information Retrieval System
PRAG	performance risk assessment group
RFI	request for information
RFP	request for proposals
RFQ	request for quotations
SBA	Small Business Administration
SDB	small disadvantaged business
SF	Standard Form
SOO	statement of objectives
SOW	statement of work
SSA	source selection authority
SSAC	source selection advisory committee/council
SSEB	source selection evaluation board
SSO	source selection official
SSP	source selection plan
TEP	technical evaluation panel
TET	technical evaluation team
UCF	uniform contract format

GLOSSARY

Acquisition. Acquiring goods or services by contract.

Acquisition cycle. FAR Part 7 lists "milestones for the acquisition cycle" that begin with acquisition plan approval and end with contract award. However, this term is sometimes used to describe events that begin with identification of a requirement and end with either contract award or delivery of the product or service.

Acquisition plan. A plan that meets the FAR Part 7 requirement that agencies perform acquisition planning for all acquisitions. Agency regulations normally establish dollar thresholds or other criteria for the requirement of written plans and assign responsibility for preparation of and approval of plans.

Acquisition team. FAR 1.102 defines an acquisition team as consisting of "all participants in Government acquisition including not only representatives of the technical, supply, and procurement communities but also the customers they serve, and the contractors who provide the products and services."

Advisory multistep process. A variation on conventional source selection procedures in which potential competitors are asked for preliminary information, on the basis of which the government advises them whether it considers them to be viable competitors for a planned source selection.

Architect-engineer (AE) services. Professional services of an architectural or engineering nature that include:
1. Services defined by state law as being AE services, or
2. Certain contract AE services associated with real property (such as research, planning, development, design, construction, alteration or repair), or
3. Other professional services of an architectural or engineering nature or incidental services that members of the architectural or engineering professions might logically or justifiably perform.

Architectural and Transportation Barriers Compliance Board (Access Board). An independent entity that formulates government positions involving access to buildings, equipment, and transportation for people with disabilities. The so-called section 508 accessibility standards for electronic and information technology (section 508 of the Rehabilitation Act Amendments of 1998) have had a particular impact on contracting.

Best and final offer (BAFO). A term formerly used to establish a common cutoff date for receipt of proposal revisions. All offerors still being considered for award were requested to submit a best and final offer by a particular date and time.

Best and really final offer (BARFO). A derisive term referring to the past government practice of obtaining multiple best and final offers in order to obtain price reductions.

Best value. The expected outcome of an acquisition that, in the government's estimation, provides the greatest overall benefit in response to the requirement. FAR Part 15 specifically addresses the lowest price, technically acceptable method of source selection and the trade-off method of source selection as ways to obtain best value.

Best value continuum. Per FAR Part 15:

> An agency can obtain best value in negotiated acquisitions by using any one or a combination of source selection approaches. In different types of acquisitions, the relative importance of cost or price may vary. For example, in acquisitions where the requirement is clearly definable and the risk of unsuccessful contract performance is minimal, cost or price may play a dominant role in source selection. The less definitive the requirement, the more development work required, or the greater the performance risk, the more technical or past performance considerations may play a dominant role in source selection.

Bid/bidder. This term usually refers to an offer from a competing contractor, or the competing contractor itself, when the procurement is conducted using the sealed bidding process described in FAR Part 12. It is sometimes used in a broader sense to mean any offer or offeror.

Broad agency announcements. Directed toward advancing the state of the art rather than focusing on specific hardware or system solutions, this method of solicitation for basic and applied research is not as constricting as conventional source selection and affords the government wide latitude in selecting sources (contractors).

Brooks Act. A government law pertaining to the selection of architects and engineers to provide services to the government.

Bundling. Consolidating two or more supply or service requirements that had previously been procured under separate contracts into a solicitation for a single contract. Sometimes, the term is used only to refer to situations where combining requirements may impact the ability of small businesses to compete.

Case law. A term often used to describe precedent established by the comptroller general or the federal courts in protest and other opinions issued by these bodies. In this book, it refers to established precedents related to source selection.

Catalog prices. Prices regularly published by businesses or otherwise available for inspection by customers.

Certificate of competency (COC). FAR Subpart 19.6 defines a COC as a certificate issued by the Small Business Administration stating that the holder is "responsible" for the purpose of receiving and performing a particular contract. See the definition of *responsible* below.

Clarifications. A contracting agency exchange with competing contractors that may take place after receipt of proposals and before contract award when it is planned to make the award without holding discussions. Clarifications give a contractor an opportunity to clarify proposal content but not to change proposal content beyond the correction of minor or clerical errors.

Combined solicitation/synopsis. A streamlining procedure described in FAR Subpart 12.6 that combines the advertising of a solicitation with the solicitation itself in a single notice at the governmentwide point of entry.

Commercial item. The definition for commercial "item" as set forth in FAR 2.101 encompasses a wide variety of items and services available (or about to become available) in the commercial marketplace.

Communications. Exchanges that may take place between the government and competing contractors after receipt of proposals but before the establishment of a competitive range. FAR Part 15 describes situations where communications *may* be held and situations where communications *must* be held.

Competition in Contracting Act. A law passed in 1984 that was designed to enhance competition within the federal agencies. Its many provisions, including the "stay provisions" or "stay rules," have had a substantial impact on the source selection process. See the definition for *stay rules* below.

Competitive range. Proposals received by the government and found to be the most highly rated, considering both cost and merit. A competitive range is selected in order to limit the number of competing contractors with which the government will hold discussions. The competitive range may be further reduced by the contracting officer for purposes of efficiency.

Comptroller General. Head of the Government Accountability Office (GAO); appointed by the President for a 15-year term. Disappointed bidders/offerors may submit protests to the GAO. Protests may be dismissed for reasons of timeliness or standing, withdrawn by the contractor, or result in an opinion by the comptroller general on the merit of the issue being protested. Comptroller general opinions are used as legal precedent by the government in conducting source selections.

Contract clause. A term or condition in a solicitation or contract that applies after contract award and is made a part of the contract. FAR-required and optional clauses are found in FAR Part 52. Individual agencies also may have required or optional clauses in their implementing regulations.

Contract specialist. A government employee in the contracting series who normally works under the supervision of a contracting officer. Unless a contract specialist is also a contracting officer, he or she may not sign contracts on behalf of the government.

Contracting office. As used in this book, an office that awards contracts and furnishes contracting services and expertise leading to the award of contracts.

Contracting officer. As used in this book, a person authorized to enter into contracts on behalf of the government. Unless some other person is named, the contracting officer is the source selection authority.

Cost analysis. FAR 1.404 defines this term as "the review and evaluation of the separate cost elements and profit in an offeror's proposal . . . and the application of judgment to determine how well the proposed costs represent what the cost of the contract should be, assuming reasonable economy and efficiency."

Cost realism analysis. FAR 15.404-1 defines *cost realism analysis* as "the process of independently reviewing and evaluating specific elements of each offeror's proposed cost estimate to determine whether the estimated proposed cost elements are realistic for the work to be performed." Cost realism analysis must be used for cost-reimbursement source selections and may be used on fixed-price contracts.

Court of Federal Claims. A U.S. court whose many responsibilities include the hearing of protests by disappointed bidders/offerors and other interested parties.

Customer. Sometimes used by contracting personnel to mean the organizational element that submits a procurement package requesting that a procurement take place. It is also used to refer to the persons or organizations that will actually use the product or service being procured.

Debriefing. When contractors are eliminated from the competition for a source selection, they are entitled to a debriefing. The content of debriefings is prescribed by law and regulation and is fully described in FAR 15.505 and FAR 15.506.

Deficiency. As defined in FAR 15.001, a *deficiency* is "a material failure of a proposal to meet a Government requirement or a combination of significant weaknesses in a proposal that increases the risk of unsuccessful performance to an unacceptable level."

Delivery order. An order for supplies placed against an established indefinite delivery contract.

Design to cost. A process wherein design and/or development contractors are charged with designing/developing products that not only meet government technical requirements but will meet not-to-exceed cost/price goals when the products that are designed/developed are ultimately procured.

Discussions. Exchanges that take place with competing contractors in the competitive range. Discussions are held in order to obtain more favorable proposals. Discussions are normally concluded when final proposal revisions are requested.

Draft request for proposals (draft RFP). A draft document in RFP format that contains some or all of the government-proposed content for the actual RFP. It is sent to prospective contractors before issuance of the actual RFP so that contractor input can be obtained in designing (some call it *building*) the actual RFP.

Earned value management system. A project management system that tracks cost, schedule, and performance accomplishments against projections.

Evaluation factors. The factors shown in the solicitation that are used to discriminate between competing contractors in a best value source selection.

Evaluation subfactors. Used to subdivide evaluation factors into smaller components. See *subfactors* below.

Exchange. Any interaction between the government and the private sector regarding a planned or ongoing negotiated acquisition. Some categories of exchanges are clarifications, communications, and discussions.

Executive agency. Any agency in the executive branch of the U.S. government.

Executive order. An order issued by the President of the United States, the head of the executive branch of the government.

Expected value. A statistical tool helpful in decision-making. As used in this book, it is a consensus probability assessment of projected success based on multiple individual assessments of past performance achievements.

Fair and reasonable price or cost. A cost or price is normally considered reasonable if it does not exceed that which would be incurred by a prudent person in the conduct of a competitive business. Proposed prices or costs are determined to be fair and reasonable through price analysis or cost analysis. In some cases probable costs and life cycle costs may be taken into consideration.

FedBizOpps. See *governmentwide point of entry*.

Federal Acquisition Regulation (FAR). The primary regulation in the Federal Acquisition Regulation System. Other parts of the system include the agency regulations that implement or supplement the FAR.

General Services Administration (GSA). A government organization with an extensive range of acquisition-related responsibilities, including the execution and management of a wide variety of task order contracts for governmentwide use.

Government Accountability Office (GAO). An independent, nonpartisan agency that works for Congress. Often called the "congressional watchdog," GAO investigates how the federal government spends taxpayer dollars. Among its broad range of responsibilities, it accepts protests from disappointed bidders or offerors and issues precedent-setting opinions.

Governmentwide point of entry (GPE). A central point where information about government business opportunities can be accessed electronically by the public. It is located at www.fedbizopps.gov or www.fbo.gov.

Head of the agency. FAR 2.101 defines the *head of the agency* as "the Secretary, Attorney General, Administrator, Governor, Chairpersons, or other chief official of an executive agency, unless otherwise indicated, including any deputy or assistant chief official of an executive agency."

Historically black college or university. Defined in the name itself, such an institution must be so determined by the Secretary of Education.

HUBZone. Historically underutilized business zone. Businesses within these areas may be entitled to preferential treatment for specific procurements.

Integrated product team (IPT). A term used by some agencies to describe the team concept used in acquisition planning and execution. The Defense Acquisition University website defines an *integrated product team* as "a multidisciplinary group of people who are collectively responsible for delivering a defined product or process."

Interested party. As used in determining eligibility to protest, an actual or prospective offeror whose direct economic interest would be affected by the award of a contract or failure to award a contract. In private–public competitions (see the definition for *outsourcing*), an interested party may be the party submitting an offer on behalf of the government. On some occasions in the past, organizations that were not competing contractors were sometimes found to be interested parties under the "economic interest" criteria. For example, a trade association might have been determined to be an interested party if a significant part of its membership would have been affected by the award or non-award of a contract.

Invitation for bids (IFB). The solicitation used in the sealed bidding method of procurement, in which only a price is submitted (unless bid samples are required) and award is made to the lowest responsive and responsible bidder, provided that the price submitted is determined to be fair and reasonable.

Item for negotiation (IFN). A proposal evaluation form used by some agencies to identify the need for exchanges with competing contractors.

Lowest price, technically acceptable (LPTA). One method of obtaining best value in source selection. Award is made to the competing contractor offering the lowest price among the acceptable proposals.

Make or buy program. A contractor's plan for a contract wherein the contractor identifies the effort to be performed in house and the work/products to be subcontracted/bought.

Market prices. Current prices in the open market that can be substantiated by competition or from sources independent of any particular offeror.

Market research. FAR Part 2 defines market research as "collecting and analyzing information about capabilities within the market to satisfy agency needs."

Merit factors. A term sometimes used to describe the non-cost factors in a source selection. Some prefer this term to *technical factors* because it encompasses technical, past performance, and management factors.

Negotiation. A method of procurement that differs from sealed bidding in that discussions are permitted and the award decision may be made based on factors other than price or cost alone. Also used in the FAR to describe "discussions" in a noncompetitive environment.

Non-cost factors. Proposal evaluation factors that are not cost or price factors.

Nondevelopmental item (NDI). Any previously developed item used or planned for use exclusively for governmental purposes by a federal agency, a state or local government, or a foreign government with which the United States has a mutual defense agreement. An NDI can also be any of those kinds of items with minor modifications of a type customarily available in the commercial marketplace.

North American Industry Classification System (NAICS). Used for classifying North American businesses for statistical purposes, the NAICS manual is used by the Small Business Administration and contracting agencies in defining what constitutes a small business for any particular acquisition of a supply or service.

Offeror. An entity that makes an offer to the government that may be accepted by the government, thus creating a contract. The term is most often used in connection with negotiated procurements.

Office of Federal Procurement Policy. Part of the Office of Management and Budget, it provides overall direction for government procurement policies. Among many other pursuits, it issues best-practices guides and chairs the Federal Acquisition Regulation Council.

Office of Government Ethics (OGE). A separate agency within the executive branch of the federal government that is responsible for establishing executive branch policies regarding conflicts of interest and other related ethical matters.

Office of Management and Budget (OMB). A Cabinet-level office, formerly known as the Bureau of the Budget, within the Executive Office of the President. It assists in preparing the federal budget and oversees the manner in which budgeted funds are expended. It issues circulars and policy letters to federal agencies with a broad range of management guidance.

Oral presentation. A presentation given by competing contractors to government evaluators in a manner specified by the provisions of a solicitation. Oral presentations may substitute for or augment written proposal information from competing contractors.

Outsourcing. As used in this book, a term that describes competitions held between the government and private contractors to determine if work that is not of an inherently governmental nature should be done by government employees or by the private sector.

Past performance. A FAR-required proposal evaluation factor that addresses how well competing contractors have performed on relevant past contracts. The contracting officer may waive the use of this factor if he or she appropriately documents the contract file to explain why past performance is not being considered.

Past Performance Information Retrieval System (PPIRS). A database of contractor past performance information.

Past performance questionnaire. An agency-prescribed form used by evaluators in obtaining past performance information from contractor-furnished points of contact or from other sources.

Performance risk assessment group (PRAG). A group established to evaluate the past performance of competing contractors and to perform a risk assessment of probable future performance based on their record of past performance.

Performance work statement. A performance-based requirements document used in solicitations and contracts. See *statement of work*.

Postaward notification. A notification to all competing contractors (except those that already received a preaward notification) that had a proposal in the competitive range but were not selected for award.

Preaward notification. The contracting officer notifies competing contractors when their proposals are excluded from the competitive range or otherwise eliminated from the competition. Preaward notification of all competing offerors is also required prior to the award of contracts that have been set aside for certain socioeconomic purposes or where a certain segment of the private sector receives a benefit for socioeconomic purposes.

Precedent. As used in this book, this term refers to guidance established when the comptroller general or the federal courts issue opinions that interpret the meaning, intent, and application of source selection laws, regulations, and policies.

Preproposal conference. A conference for competing contractors that is conducted by the government after a solicitation has been issued but before proposals are due. The contents of the solicitation are reviewed, and the government answers any questions competing contractors may have.

Presolicitation conference. A conference for potential offerors that is held by the government before a solicitation is issued to both inform and gather input from the private sector. Where appropriate, contractor feedback may be reflected in the solicitation.

Presolicitation exchange. Any communication that is held with prospective contractors before a solicitation (such as a request for proposal) is issued.

Price analysis. The process of examining and evaluating a proposed price without evaluating the separate cost elements and profit that make up the price. It is used to determine if prices received are fair and reasonable. The government compares a proposed price with such things as other prices received for the same or similar products or services in the past, prices offered or bid by competitors, catalog prices, government estimates, or other benchmarks.

Probable cost. Cost realism analysis is used to adjust a contractor's proposed cost to reflect what the cost probably will be. These government-estimated costs are called *probable costs* and are used in lieu of proposed costs when evaluating proposals to determine best value whenever a cost-reimbursement contract is contemplated. Probable costs may be used in source selections for fixed-price contracts in assessing risk and determining contractor responsibility.

Procurement administrative lead time (PALT). Generally, the time from receipt of an acceptable procurement request at the government contracting office until the time a contract award is made.

Program office. As used in this book, the government office responsible for a program requirement that will be met through the use of a contract.

Program officer. As used in this book, the individual who has been assigned primary responsibility for a program requirement that will be met through the use of a contract.

Proposals. Contractor submissions in response to a request for proposal.

Proposal evaluation board (PEB). A term used by some agencies to describe a group established to evaluate the proposals of competing contractors.

Proposal revision. A revision to a contractor-submitted proposal. Once the closing date for receipt of proposals has passed, proposals may be revised only when permitted or directed by the contracting officer. At the conclusion of any discussions, contractors are given the opportunity to submit a final proposal revision by a specified time and date.

Protest. As defined in FAR Part 33, a *protest* is a written objection by an interested party to any of the following:
- A solicitation or other request by an agency for offers for a contract for the procurement of property or services
- The cancellation of the solicitation or other request
- An award or proposed award of the contract
- A termination or cancellation of an award of the contract, if the written objection contains an allegation that the termination or cancellation is based in whole or in part on improprieties concerning the award of the contract.

Quality. An attribute that, according to FAR 15.304, must be addressed in every source selection and can be determined through factors such as an offeror's past performance, compliance with solicitation requirements, technical excellence, management capability, personnel qualifications, and prior experience.

Quote. A contractor submission in response to a request for quotations.

Quoter. An entity that submits a quote to the government rather than submitting an offer. This means that the government must subsequently make an offer to buy that is accepted by the quoter, either by signature or by performance.

Rating methodology. The manner in which proposals are scored or rated. In the most common rating methods, numerical scores, adjectival ratings, or color ratings are assigned to the non-cost evaluation factors and subfactors in each proposal.

Rating proposals. Categorizing the relative quality of proposals to help determine best value. For example, one or more proposals could be categorized as "outstanding," while others might be "acceptable" or "marginal."

Responsible/responsibility. To obtain a contract, a contractor must be found to be responsible by the contracting officer. This determination of responsibility is based upon (1) an assessment of the contractor's ability to perform and (2) an assessment of the contractor's will to perform as demonstrated by past performance.

Responsive/responsiveness. To obtain a contract, a contractor must be deemed to be responsive. This means that the contractor must comply with solicitation instructions and must not take exception to the government's requirements as described in the solicitation.

Representations and certifications. Solicitation provisions require that the contractor certify or represent various matters that may pertain to its eligibility to receive an award or that help the government obtain business-related statistics. For example, a contractor could represent its status as a woman-owned small business. FAR 4.1201 requires that contractors complete annual certifications and representations electronically.

Request for information (RFI). A document that is used to obtain information when the government has no immediate plan to award a contract but wants to obtain private-sector input for planning purposes. Unless specified by individual agencies, there is no required format for RFIs.

Request for proposals (RFP). The solicitation normally used for negotiated procurements under FAR Part 15, including best value source selections.

Request for quotations (RFQ). The solicitation often used for simplified acquisitions (as described in FAR Part 13) and sometimes used for competitions between task order contract holders.

Requirements document. The document that tells contractors what the government will require them to do under the contract. The various types of requirements documents include purchase descriptions, statements of work, and statements of objectives.

Reverse auctioning. A procurement technique whereby bidders' prices are disclosed to other bidders, who may then offer a lower price. Reverse auctioning has been most typically used in government for information technology–related procurements.

Sample-itis. A term used in this book to refer to the practice of preparing new solicitations by copying previous solicitations rather than tailoring the solicitation to the requirement at hand.

Scoring proposals. See *rating proposals*. These terms are generally used as synonyms.

Service-disabled veteran-owned small business concern. A small business for which at least 51 percent of the ownership is held by one or more veterans with a service-connected disability and where daily operations are controlled by the veteran(s). If the veteran(s) has or have a permanent and severe disability, daily business operations can be controlled by a spouse or permanent caregiver.

Should cost. A method of cost analysis in which the government evaluates the economy and efficiency of the contractor's operations, rather than assuming that historical costs reflect efficient and economical operation.

Significant weakness. As defined in FAR 15.001, a *significant weakness* in a proposal is a flaw that appreciably increases the risk of unsuccessful performance.

Simplified acquisition. A procurement executed using the provisions of FAR Part 13. At times agencies use best value source selection procedures for simplified acquisitions.

Simplified acquisition thresholds. The dollar limitations for use of FAR Part 13 procedures.

Site visit. When work under a contemplated contract is to be performed at a location other than contractor or subcontractor locations (for example, if work is to be performed at a government location), competing contractors may be invited to visit the site before submitting proposals.

Small business. A business concern that is independently owned and operated, is not dominant in the field of operation in which it is bidding on a government contract, and meets size standards established by the Small Business Administration (SBA). The SBA publishes these standards in the *North American Industry Classification System Manual*.

Small Business Administration (SBA). The SBA counsels and assists small business concerns and helps government contracting personnel ensure that small business concerns, including small disadvantaged businesses, veteran-owned businesses, businesses located in HUBZones, and others, receive a fair proportion of contracts for supplies and services.

Small business size standards. Standards established by the Small Business Administration and published in the *North American Industry Classification System Manual*. Differing standards exist for differing segments of industry.

Small disadvantaged business. A small business concern that is owned by one or more "disadvantaged individuals." A disadvantaged individual is a person who is socially or economically disadvantaged by virtue of his or her identification with a particular group. (A more detailed description can be found at FAR 2.101.) Normally, small disadvantaged businesses seek certification from the Small Business Administration to receive preferential treatment.

Solicitation. Any request inviting potential contractors to submit a bid, offer, or quotation. Solicitations under sealed bid procedures are called invitations for bids. With few exceptions, solicitations under negotiated procedures are called requests for proposals. Solicitations under simplified acquisition procedures can require submission of either a quote or an offer. Often, a request for quotations is used for simplified acquisitions.

Solicitation provision. A provision of a solicitation that pertains only to the solicitation and not to any resultant contract. One example is the *Instructions to Offerors—Competitive Acquisitions* provision that is found in FAR Part 52 and used in competitive negotiated procurements.

Source selection advisory council (SSAC). A group established to oversee the operations of proposal evaluation groups (such as the source selection evaluation board) and to advise the source selection authority on matters such as establishing the competitive range and selecting a source.

Source selection authority (SSA). The government employee with the responsibility to select the source (or sources) whose proposal(s) represents the best value for the government. The contracting officer acts as the SSA unless the agency head appoints another person for a specific acquisition or a group of acquisitions.

Source selection decision. An independent decision made by the source selection authority as to which contractor(s) will receive a contract at the conclusion of a particular source selection process. The rationale for the decision must be documented.

Source selection evaluation board (SSEB). A board established to evaluate proposals from competing contractors.

Source selection information. Information that must be protected under the Procurement Integrity Act. It may include pricing, proprietary information, and ranking of offerors.

Source selection official (SSO). Term sometimes used interchangeably with *source selection authority*; also sometimes used to refer to any official involved in the source selection process.

Source selection plan. A term used by many agencies to describe the document that contains particulars about the planned process to obtain best value, including the overall source selection strategy. Agency regulations normally assign responsibility for plan preparation and plan approval.

Statement of objectives (SOO). A government-prepared requirements document that is incorporated into the solicitation and identifies overall performance objectives. It is used in solicitations where the government intends to provide the maximum flexibility for each offeror to propose an innovative approach to meeting the government's performance requirements.

Statement of work (SOW). A requirements document that addresses what a contractor is supposed to accomplish under the contract. It may be design based, which means the government tells the contractor how to do the work, or performance based, which means the government identifies the work required without giving "how-to" instructions. When the statement of work is performance based, it is usually called a *performance work statement*.

Stay provisions/stay rules. Portions of the Competition in Contracting Act that provide that an agency must (except under very limited circumstances) delay award if it receives a protest before award or must suspend contract performance if it receives a protest after award. In the latter case, the stay provisions apply only if the protest was received within ten days after the contract was awarded or received within five days after a debriefing date offered to the protestor.

Streamlined solicitation for commercial items. This procedure allows for combining the synopsis and the solicitation into one entry at the governmentwide point of entry. See FAR Subpart 12.6 for instructions for using the procedure.

Subfactors. Evaluation factors in a government solicitation may be subdivided into subfactors to emphasize certain aspects of the factors or to facilitate proposal preparation and evaluation.

Synopsis. A brief description of a proposed contract action or award. With some exceptions, the government is required to publicize proposed contract actions by describing (synopsizing) them in the governmentwide point of entry. With certain exceptions, contract awards also must be synopsized in the governmentwide point of entry.

Task order. A delivery order under at a task order contract.

Task order contract. An indefinite delivery contract for services. Quite often, a task order contract is an indefinite delivery/indefinite quantity contract with a specified minimum and maximum amount.

Technical analysis. An analysis of proposal costs by people with specialized engineering, science, or management skills to determine if the labor hours, categories of labor, material, scrap rates, and other such matters detailed in a proposal are reasonable.

Technical evaluation team (TET) or panel (TEP). A group established to evaluate the non-cost aspects of proposals.

Technical factors. A term sometimes used to refer to the non-cost factors in a best value source selection. Some agencies make a distinction between technical factors and management factors when using this term whereas others do not.

Technical personnel. A term used in the FAR to describe people on an acquisition team who are not contracting personnel, users, supply personnel, or customers. The term is often used to describe scientific, engineering, or other people whose occupation deals with the sciences.

Trade-off. One method of obtaining best value in source selection. It permits trade-offs among cost or price and non-cost factors and allows the government to accept other than the lowest-priced proposal.

Value analysis. A technique used as a part of price or cost analysis to determine the value of a cost or service that may include factors other than just the proposed cost or price—for example, life cycle costs, such as the costs of operation and disposal.

Veteran-owned small business. A small business that is majority-owned (51 percent or more) by veterans and whose management and daily operations are controlled by one or more veterans.

Weakness. As defined in FAR 15.001, a flaw in a proposal that increases the risk of unsuccessful contract performance.

Woman-owned small business. A small business that is majority-owned (51 percent or more) by one or more women and whose management and daily operations are controlled by one or more women.

INDEX

A

acquisition plan (AP), 15–20
acquisition strategy, reaching consensus, 3–4
actual user, 2
adjectival ratings, 57
adverse past performance information, 126
advisors, 29–31, 95–98
advisory multistep selection process, 157
AE. *See* architect-engineer services
agency legal counsel, 2
agency small business advisor, 2
AP. *See* acquisition plan
arbitrary cutoff points, 119
architect-engineer (AE) services, 157–159
attendees, oral presentations, 73
attorney fees, 25
auctioning, 131
awards, 116–117

B

BAA. *See* broad agency announcement
best and final offer (BAFO), 136
best and really final offer (BARFO), 136
best value, 6
bid and proposal costs, 25
broad agency announcement (BAA), 160–161

C

certificate of competency (COC), 63
CICA. *See* Competition in Contracting Act
clarifications, 115–116
COC. *See* certificate of competency
color ratings, 57
commercial item procurement, 159–160
communications, 123–124
competence and fairness, 31–32
Competition in Contracting Act (CICA), 21
competitive range, 119–121
competitive source selections, 5–6
conferences, 38
contract awards, 116–117
contracting officer, 2, 28
contractors, 3, 21, 37–40
cost, 65–66
cost analysis, 109–113
cost and price exchanges, limits on, 132–133
cost realism, 110–111

D

debriefings
  face-to-face, 150
  format, 150
  information that may not be furnished, 149
  lessons learned, 150
  postaward, 148
  preaward, 147–148
  responses to relevant questions, 149
deficiencies, 126–127
discussions, 125–129, 135–136
draft request for proposals, 38

E

equipment, oral presentations, 73
ethics
  avoiding appearance of impropriety, 164
  principles for government employees, 163, 165–168
  Procurement Integrity Act, 163

evaluating merit
  agency forms, 102
  beginning proposal evaluations, 99
  retaining evaluators and evaluation forms, 102–103
  small business subcontracting plans, 103
  typical evaluation process, 99–102
evaluation factors
  FAR requirements, 41–42
  impact, 44
  non-cost factors, 42–44
  relative importance, 53–56
  subfactors, 42, 51–52
evaluators, 28–31, 95–98
extraordinary contractor rights, 21

F

face-to-face debriefings, 150
FAR. See Federal Acquisition Regulation
FASA. See Federal Acquisition Streamlining Act
favoring, 132
FedBizOpps, 157, 160–161
Federal Acquisition Regulation (FAR), 1
Federal Acquisition Streamlining Act (FASA), 153
formal versus other than formal source selections, 28–29

G

government point of entry (GPE), 7–9

I

indefinite delivery/indefinite quantity (ID/IQ), 154
interested party, 22–23

L

lessons learned, 150
location, oral presentations, 73

lowest price, technically acceptable (LPTA)
  best value, 6
  definition, 5
  trade-off, compared to, 11–14

M

market research, 33–35, 69–70
media, 68
merit factors, 41

N

negotiations, 125
notification to offerors, 145–146
numerical weights, 57

O

ombudsman, 155
one-on-one meetings, 39
oral presentations, 71–74
ordinal ratings, 57
override procedures, 21–22

P

past performance
  evaluating, 105–107
  importance, 61–64
  using information about, 133
postaward debriefings, 148
preaward debriefings, 147–148
preproposal conferences, 89–93
presolicitation exchanges, 37–40
price analysis, 109–113
Procurement Integrity Act, 163
program office, 1
prohibited exchanges, 131–134
project office, 1
proposal evaluation board. See evaluators
proposal preparation instructions, 67–70
proprietary information, 132

protests, 21–26
public hearings, 38

R

rating methods, 57–60
recording oral presentations, 73
relative importance, evaluation factors, 53–56
request for information (RFI), 7–8, 38
request for proposal (RFP), 9, 38
rescheduling oral presentations, 73
revisions, 135–137
RFI. *See* request for information
RFP. *See* request for proposal

S

sample-itis, 44
SBA. *See* Small Business Administration
SDB. *See* small disadvantaged business
Section L example, 169–177
Section M example, 177–184
short list, 119
significant weaknesses, 126
simple tasks, 154
Small Business Administration (SBA), 63
small business subcontracting plans, 103
small businesses, 47–49
small disadvantaged business (SDB), 48–49, 64
socioeconomic evaluation factors, 49
sole source versus competition, 5
solicitation preparation
　compatibility and clarity, 80–81
　instructions to offerors, 80, 83–88
　special standards, 81
　uniform contract format, 79, 82
source selection advisory council (SSAC), 29
source selection authority (SSA)
　contracting officer, 28
　duties, 27–28
　importance of, 3, 11–12

source selection decision, 139–143
source selection evaluation board (SSEB), 29
source selection information, protecting, 133
source selection plan (SSP), 16–20
source selection process overview, 6–10
SSA. *See* source selection authority
SSAC. *See* source selection advisory council
SSEB. *See* source selection evaluation board
SSP. *See* source selection plan
stakeholders, 1–2
stay provisions, 21
subfactors, 42, 51–52
synopsis, 75–78

T

task order contracts, 153–156
technical evaluation panel. *See* evaluators
technical evaluation team. *See* evaluators
technical leveling, 131
technical transfusion, 131
time of evaluation, oral presentations, 73
trade-off procurement, sample evaluation form, 97–98
trade-off source selection, 11–14

U

unacceptable proposals, 120
uniform contract format (UCF), 79, 159

V

volumes, 68

W

weaknesses, proposal, 126–127